Don't You Know Anybody Else?

family stories by
Ted Allan

McClelland and Stewart

To KATE, who helped start a new family
I can write about next.

Copyright © 1985 by Ted Allan

The Canadian Publishers
McClelland and Stewart Limited
25 Hollinger Road, Toronto M4B 3G2

Canadian Cataloguing in Publication Data
Allan, Ted.
  Don't you know anybody else?
ISBN 0-7710-0728-0
I. Title.
PS8551.L54D66 1985 C813'.54 C85-098325-8
PR9199.3.A55D66 1985

Typography and assembly by The Literary Service,
Toronto, Ontario

Printed and bound in Canada by Webcom Limited

Also by Ted Allan

Books
This Time a Better Earth, 1940
The Scalpel, The Sword, The Story of
    Dr. Norman Bethune (co-author), 1954
Quest for Pajaro, 1970
Willie, the Squowse, 1978, 1984
Love Is a Long Shot, 1984

Films
Lies My Father Told Me, 1976
Falling in Love Again, 1981
It Rained All Night, 1981
Love Streams, 1984

Plays
The Money Makers, 1956
Gog and Magog, 1959
    (with Roger MacDougall)
Legend of Paradiso, 1959
The Secret of the World, 1962
Oh What a Lovely War (stage treatment), 1964
Chu Chem a Zen Buddhist Hebrew Musical, 1968
I've Seen You Cut Lemons, 1970
Love Streams, 1982
The Third Day Comes, 1982
Everyone Else, a Stranger, 1984
Lies My Father Told Me, 1984

Acknowledgements

"Lies My Father Told Me" first appeared in 1949 in the *Canadian Jewish Congress Bulletin* under the title of "My Zaida." It has subsequently appeared in many anthologies and has been broadcast over the CBC and BBC a few times since 1951.

"Looking for Bessie" first appeared in the *New Yorker* in 1944 and was also read on the CBC and BBC.

"Big Boys Shouldn't Cry" was first published in the *New Yorker* in 1947 and was read a number of times on the CBC and BBC.

All the other stories were broadcast, in slightly different form, on CBC's "Anthology" series during the sixties, seventies and eighties.

Contents

Lies My Father Told Me

MY GRANDFATHER STOOD SIX FEET THREE IN HIS worn-out slippers. He had a long grey beard with streaks of white running through it. When he prayed, his voice boomed like a choir as he turned the pages of his prayer book with one hand and stroked his beard with the other. His hands were bony and looked like tree roots; they were powerful. My grandpa had been a farmer in the old country. In Montreal he conducted what he called "a second-hand business."

In his youth, I was told, Grandpa had been something of a wild man, drinking and playing with the village wenches until my grandmother took him in hand. In his old age, when I knew him, he had become a very religious man. He prayed three times a day on weekdays and all day on Saturday. In between prayers he rode around on a wagon which, as I look back, rolled on despite all the laws of physics and mechanics. Its four wheels always seemed to be going in every direction but forwards. The horse that pulled the wagon was called Ferdeleh. He was my pet and it was only much later, when I had seen many other horses, that I realized that Ferdeleh was not everything a horse could have been. His belly hung very low, almost touching the street when he walked. His head went back and forth in

9

jerky motions in complete disharmony with the rest of him. He moved slowly, almost painfully, apparently realizing that he was capable of only one speed and determined to go no faster or slower than the rate he had established some time back. Next to Grandpa I loved Ferdeleh best, with the possible exception of God, or my mother when she bought me candy.

On Sundays when it didn't rain, Grandpa, Ferdeleh and I would go riding through the back lanes of Montreal. The lanes then were not paved as they are now, and after a rainy Saturday, the mud would be inches deep and the wagon heaved and shook like a barge in a stormy sea. Ferdeleh's pace remained, as always, the same. He liked the mud. It was easy on his feet.

When the sun shone through my window on Sunday morning, I would jump out of bed, wash, dress, run into the kitchen where Grandpa and I said our morning prayers, and then we'd both go to harness and feed Ferdeleh. On Sundays Ferdeleh would whinny like a happy child. He knew it was an extra special day for all of us. By the time he had finished his oats and hay, Grandpa and I would be finished with our breakfast which Grandma and Mother had prepared for us.

Then we'd go through what Grandpa called "the women's Sunday song." It went like this: "Don't let him hold the reins crossing streets. Be sure to come back if it starts to rain." They would repeat this about three hundred times until Grandpa and I were weary from nodding our heads and saying "Yes." We could hear it until we turned the corner and went up the lane of the next street.

Then began the most wonderful of days as we drove through the dirt lanes of Montreal, skirting the garbage cans, jolting and bouncing through the mud and dust, calling every cat by name and every cat meowing its hello, and Grandpa and I holding our hands to our ears and shouting out at the top of our lungs, "Rags, cloze, botels! Rags, cloze, botels!"

What a wonderful game that was! I would run up the back stairs and bring back all kinds of fascinating things — old dresses, suits, pants, rags, newspapers, all shapes of bottles, all shapes of trash, everything you could think of, until the wagon was filled.

Sometimes a woman would ask me to send Grandpa up to give her a price on what she had, and Grandpa would shout up from downstairs, "My feet ache. The boy will give you the price." I knew what he offered for an old suit, for an old dress, and I would shout down describing the items in question and the state of deterioration. For clothes that were nothing better than rags, we offered a standard price, "Fifteen cents, take it or leave it." Clothes that might be repaired I would hold out for Grandpa to see and he'd appraise it. And so we'd go through the lanes of the city.

Sometimes the women would not be satisfied with the money Grandpa had given me for them. Grandpa would always say, "Eleshka, women always want more than they get. Remember that. Give them a brick and they want the whole house."

My Sunday rides were the happiest times I spent. Sometimes Grandpa would let me wear his derby hat which came down over my ears, and people would look at me and laugh and I'd feel even happier feeling how happy everyone was on Sunday.

Sometimes strange, wonderful smells would come over the city, muffling the smell of the garbage cans. When this happened we would stop Ferdeleh and breathe deeply. It smelled of sea and of oak trees and flowers.

Then we knew we were near the mountain in the centre of the city and that the wind from the river was bringing the perfumes of the mountain and spraying it over the city. Often we would ride out of the back lanes and ride up the mountain road. We couldn't go too far up because it was a strain on Ferdeleh. As far as we went, surrounded on each side by tall poplars and evergreens, Grandpa would tell me about the old country, about the rivers and the farms, and sometimes he'd get off the wagon and pick up some black earth in his hands. He'd squat, letting the earth fall between his fingers, and I'd squat beside him doing the same thing.

When we came to the mountain, Grandpa's mood would change and he would talk to me of the great land that Canada was, and of the great things the young people growing up were going to do in this great land. Ferdeleh would walk to the edge of the road and eat the thick grass on the sides. Grandpa was at home among the trees and black earth and thick grass, and on our way down the mountain road he would sing songs that weren't prayers, but happy songs in Russian. Sometimes he'd clap his hands to the song as I held the reins and Ferdeleh would look back at him and shake his head with pleasure.

One Sunday on our ride home through the mountain, a group of young boys and girls threw stones at us and shouted in French, *"Juif... Juif..."* Grandpa held his strong arm around me, cursed back, muttering "anti-Semites" under his breath. When I asked him what he said, he answered, "It is something I hope you never learn." The boys and girls laughed and got tired of throwing stones. That was the last Sunday we went to the mountain.

If it rained on Sunday my mother wouldn't let me go out, so every Saturday evening I prayed for the sun to shine on Sunday. Once I almost lost faith in God and in the power of prayer. For three Sundays in succession it rained. In my desperation I took it out on God. What was the use of praying to Him if he didn't listen to you? I complained to Grandpa.

"Perhaps you don't pray right," he suggested.

"But I do. I say, 'Our God in heaven, hallowed by Thy name, Thy will on earth as it is in heaven. Please don't let it rain tomorrow.' "

"Ah! In English you pray?" my grandfather exclaimed triumphantly.

"Yes," I answered.

"But God only answers prayers in Hebrew. I will teach you how to say that prayer in Hebrew. And if God doesn't answer, it's your own fault. He's angry because you didn't use the Holy Language."

But God wasn't angry because next Sunday the sun shone its brightest and the three of us went for our Sunday ride.

On weekdays, when Grandpa and I arose a little after daybreak and said our morning prayers, I would mimic his sing-song lamentations, sounding as if my heart were breaking and wondering why we both had to sound so sad. I must have put everything I had into it because Grandpa assured me that one day I would become a great cantor and a leader of the Hebrews. "You will sing so that the ocean will open up a path before you and you will lead our people to a new paradise."

I was six then and he was the only man I ever understood even when I didn't understand his words. I learned a lot from him. If he didn't learn a lot from me, he made me feel he did.

I remember once saying, "You know, sometimes I think I'm the son of God. Is it possible?"

"It is possible," he answered, "but don't rely on it. Many of us are sons of God. The important thing is not to rely too much upon it. The harder we work, the harder we study, the more we accomplish, the surer we are that we are sons of God."

At the synagogue on Saturday his old, white-bearded

friends would surround me and ask me questions. Grandpa would stand by and burst with pride. I strutted like a peacock.

"Who is David?" the old man would ask me.

"He's the man with the beard, the man with the bearded words." And they laughed.

"And who is God?" they would ask me.

"King and creator of the Universe, the all-powerful one, the almighty one, more powerful even than Grandpa." They laughed again and I thought I was pretty smart. So did Grandpa. So did my grandmother and my mother.

So did everyone, except my father. I didn't like my father. He said things to me like, "For God's sake, you're smart, but not as smart as you think. Nobody is that smart." He was jealous of me and he told me lies. He told me lies about Ferdeleh.

"Ferdeleh is one part horse, one part camel and one part chicken," he told me.

Grandpa told me that was a lie, Ferdeleh was all horse. "If he is part of anything, he is part human," said Grandpa.

I agreed with him. Ferdeleh understood everything we said to him. No matter what part of the city he was in, he could find his way home, even in the dark.

"Ferdeleh is going to collapse one day in one heap," my father said. "Ferdeleh is carrying twins. . . . Ferdeleh is going to keel over one day and die. . . . He should be shot now or he'll collapse under you one of these days," my father would say.

Neither Grandpa nor I had much use for the opinions of my father.

On top of everything, my father had no beard, didn't pray, didn't go to synagogue on the Sabbath, read English books and never read the prayer books, played piano on the Sabbath and sometimes would draw my mother into his villainies by making her sing while he played. On the

Sabbath this was an abomination to both Grandpa and me.

One day I told my father, "Papa, you have forsaken your forefathers." He burst out laughing and kissed me and then my mother kissed me, which infuriated me all the more.

I could forgive my father for not treating me as an equal, but I couldn't forgive his lies about Ferdeleh. Once he said that Ferdeleh "smelled up" the whole house and demanded that Grandpa move the stable. It was true that the kitchen, being next to the stable which was in the back shed, did sometimes smell of hay and manure, but as Grandpa said, "What is wrong with such a smell? It is a good, healthy smell."

It was a house divided, with my grandmother, mother and father on one side, and Grandpa, Ferdeleh and me on the other. One day a man came to the house and said he was from the Board of Health and that the neighbours had complained about the stable. Grandpa and I knew we were beaten then. You could get around the Board of Health, Grandpa informed me, if you could grease the palms of the officials. I suggested the obvious, but Grandpa explained that this type of "grease" was made of gold. The stable would have to be moved. But where?

As it turned out, Grandpa didn't have to worry about it. The whole matter was taken out of his hands a few weeks later.

Next Sunday the sun shone brightly and I ran to the kitchen to say my prayers with Grandpa. But Grandpa wasn't there. I found my grandmother there instead — weeping. Grandpa was in his room, ill. He had a sickness they called diabetes and at that time the only thing you could do about diabetes was weep. I fed Ferdeleh and soothed him because I knew how disappointed he was.

That week I was taken to an aunt of mine. There was no explanation given. My parents thought I was too young to need any explanations. On Saturday next I was brought home, too late to see Grandpa that evening, but I felt good knowing that I would spend the next day with him and Ferdeleh again.

When I came to the kitchen Sunday morning, Grandpa was not there. Ferdeleh was not in the stable. I thought they were playing a joke on me so I rushed to the front of the house expecting to see Grandpa sitting atop the wagon waiting for me.

But there wasn't any wagon. My father came up behind me and put his hand on my head. I looked up questioningly and he said, "Grandpa and Ferdeleh have gone to heaven..."

When he told me they were *never* coming back, I moved away from him and went to my room. I lay down on my bed and cried, not for Grandpa and Ferdeleh, because I knew they would never do such a thing to me, but for my father, because he had told me such a horrible lie.

When My Uncle Was the Messiah

THE DAY MY UNCLE BENNY WAS TOLD BY THE
Lord that he was the Messiah began like any other day.
There was, as he recalled, nothing special about it. He
awoke at six o'clock as usual, looked at his sleeping wife,
Rifka, as he always did, sighed the same sigh he always
sighed when he looked at her, washed, dressed, prayed and
went to the stable to feed his horse, before eating breakfast
and setting off for the ice factory.

During summers Uncle Benny sold ice. During winters
he sold coal. In either season he had to be in good physical
shape because both the ice and the coal were heavy to
carry. All my other uncles, my mother's brothers, were of
average height, but Benny was shorter than my mother,
who was only five feet three.

His wife was at least a head taller, and very fat, so they
looked incongruous the few times they walked together.
Their children — Moe, Bertha and Shaindel — were of average
height. Because of his size, my mother nicknamed him
"Tootsie." He was her eldest brother. I called him either
Uncle Benny or Uncle Tootsie. He didn't seem to mind,
either way. He was very good-natured about everything and
I can't remember him ever getting angry or even irritable.
This was unusual in a family which was given to quick
tempers and loud shouting.

Auntie Rifka wasn't only fat. My mother said she was "touched in the head." I never knew what that meant exactly but it seemed to have affected her first and third children, Moe and Shaindel. They never learned how to read or write, and were described by more literate members of our family as "mentally retarded." Only the middle child, Bertha, was normal like the rest of us.

None of this prevented them from being cheerful and good-natured. I liked them all. I enjoyed when they visited and I enjoyed visiting them. I was around five at the time, Moe was probably twenty and Shaindel fifteen, but we played together as if we were all the same age.

Auntie Rifka never said very much but she smiled a lot. I liked that. She often forgot to cook meals or clean up the house, but Uncle Benny never complained. He treated her as if she was one of his children rather than his wife.

There was nothing all that unusual about Uncle Benny until the day when he was in his stable and he heard a voice speaking in English — not Yiddish or Hebrew, but Montreal English — which he knew instantly to be the voice of God.

Up until that moment Uncle Benny had not been highly religious. My grandfather, his father, was a member of a Chassidic sect, although I realized later he wasn't all that orthodox, but Grandpa prayed and danced and sang a lot. I associated that with religion. Uncle Benny didn't go in for that sort of thing but he too could quote from the Talmud, the Torah, the Midrash, the Commentaries, and tell Chassidic stories. In those days — the 1920s — all my uncles were learned enough to do that, but none had ever been addressed directly by God, as had Uncle Benny.

He was forty-nine years old at the time, had just finished feeding his horse and was about to hitch him to the wagon when God spoke. "Benny," he said, "you are the Messiah."

At first Uncle Benny wasn't sure he had heard it right.

18

"What?" he asked, looking up. The voice had come from above the stable roof. Uncle Benny realized it was coming from heaven. "You, Benny," said the voice again, "are the Messiah."

Uncle Benny walked out of the stable and looked towards heaven. The voice spoke again. "I have been looking for you for many years, Benny. I meant to tell you when you were still a young man but I kept losing track of you. It's not too late. Now that you know you're the Son of God, you'll know what to do."

Uncle Benny looked around to see if anyone else had heard. The words had been distinct. There could be no mistaking them.

He heaved a sigh. "Is this your idea of a joke?" he asked the Lord. "Making *me* the Messiah? I'm just a simple man, I have two mentally backward children, and I'm not that sure about my wife either."

"That has nothing to do with it, Benny," replied God. "You are the Messiah. You will now lead humanity to peace and harmony. The world has been waiting for you for a long time."

Uncle Benny shook his head. This was a sad joke on the world. "If I am what the world's been waiting for, it's not funny," he said. He looked towards heaven again. "What am I supposed to do?" he asked, but God had moved away and didn't answer.

When Benny returned to the house, his wife could see he was disturbed about something. She asked if the horse was sick. "It's worse than that," he told her. "It turns out that I'm the Messiah."

Auntie Rifka smiled, but that wasn't unusual for her, and served him breakfast. "Are you taking Moe to help you today?" she asked.

"If he wants to come," said Benny.

"He's sleeping," said Rifka.

"Then let him sleep," said Benny. "Did you hear what I told you?"

"The horse isn't sick."

"I'm the Messiah. The Lord just told me. Me. Benny Elias. The Messiah. It's ridiculous."

"I'll go wake Moe," said Rifka, and left to do that.

Benny realized that his wife had not fully understood what he had told her, but he knew that in time she would, so he let it rest.

When Moe appeared drowsy-eyed for breakfast, Benny told him the news. "I'm the Messiah," he said. "God told me while I was in the stable."

"What are you going to do about it?" Moe had the wit to ask.

"I don't know. That's just it. I don't know what to do about it. I'll ask Bertha."

Bertha was the cleverest of them, and the whole family always deferred to her whenever a problem arose. She was a secretary for a large insurance company and went to work later than they did, so they waited for her to wake up and come to breakfast. Uncle Benny told her what had happened and asked what she thought he should do.

"While you were in the stable," she repeated, "you heard this voice and you knew it was God speaking to you."

Benny nodded. "Who else would it be, saying a thing like that and sounding like that, with a deep bass voice: 'Benny, you are the Messiah.'"

"In English?"

"In English."

"Not in Hebrew?"

"English. Plain English."

Bertha looked at her father and decided he was hallucinating. "You imagined it," she said. "Don't worry about it."

"God told me I'd know what to do. I was to bring peace and harmony to humanity."

"It's a hallucination," said his bright daughter Bertha. "You just imagined it."

"No." Uncle Benny knew he hadn't imagined it. "I heard God's voice as plain as I hear you."

Uncle Benny had to deliver ice that day, Messiah or not. He and Moe went to the factory in the north end of the city and did their rounds delivering ice to regular customers, shouting, "Ice! Ice! Ice!" to attract new customers. As they moved slowly through the streets, hosts of kids would take turns jumping onto the rear platform of the wagon for a short ride. I doubt if there was a kid in that area of the city who didn't know my Uncle Benny and my cousin Moe.

But on that particular day no one knew about his being the Messiah because he didn't mention it to anyone. He didn't know how to perform miracles or do anything else a Messiah is supposed to know how to do, so he figured the best thing was to stay silent until he talked the matter over with his father, my grandfather.

In the evening he came to visit and told Grandpa and my mother. I was in the kitchen listening as he related how God had spoken to him, what he said to God, what he said to Rifka, what Rifka said to him, what he said to Bertha and what Bertha said to him.

Grandpa listened very closely. My mother let out a soft "oi" which meant she thought Uncle Benny was now also touched in the head, but my grandfather didn't seem to think so.

"If you're the Messiah, you are going to give up your business?" he asked.

"I don't know," replied Benny. "How will my family eat if I give up the business?"

"Does the Messiah have to worry about his family eating?" Grandpa asked.

"It looks that way," said Uncle Benny.

Grandpa acknowledged the logic of this with a nod. He

could give no big advice except to say, "Wait and see what happens. God might speak to you again and tell you what to do. In the meantime," he advised, "I wouldn't tell too many people about it. Keep it a secret until God speaks to you again."

But you couldn't keep a thing like that a secret for very long. Word got out, and three wise rabbis came to investigate, calling at Uncle Benny's house to ask him questions and to make a pronouncement: was he or was he not the Messiah?

The first rabbi, very learned and orthodox, asked difficult questions about the Talmud and the Torah and the Commentaries. Benny didn't make out so good and got the answers all mixed up, saying something was from the Torah when it was from the Talmud, and attributing quotations to Jeremiah when they belonged to Isaiah. It was obvious, said the first rabbi, that Benny was not the Messiah.

The second wise rabbi was a Chassid and he asked questions pertaining to Benny's orthodoxy and strict observance of the laws. Benny didn't do too well in this department either, but as he happened to know a lot of Chassidic stories, the second rabbi didn't give a categorical no like the first one, but a "Maybe."

The third rabbi asked Benny: "If you are the Messiah, precisely what are you planning to do about bringing peace and harmony to the world?"

"I'm not sure," Benny answered, "but I thought maybe I should tell people to be nice to each other. Something like that."

This got the third rabbi excited because it sounded like authentic Messiah talk. His verdict was "Possible."

For a time Benny told his customers and other people that they should be nice to one another, but nobody paid any attention, so he became discouraged and stopped saying it.

God never spoke to Uncle Benny again and I asked my grandfather about this. His opinion was that God obviously figured Uncle Benny would know what to do once he informed him he was the Messiah.

By now the penny had started to drop with Rifka and she asked Bertha about it. Bertha explained what a Messiah was supposed to do, and Rifka began nagging Benny, saying, "You're the Messiah. You're supposed to bring peace and harmony. God told you to! Go and do it!"

Benny would shrug and say, "I know he told me, but I don't know what to do."

Rifka would say, "A Messiah who's the real Messiah would know what to do."

"Maybe I'm not the real Messiah," Uncle Benny would say, "but how could God have made such a mistake?"

But a mistake God did make, for Uncle Benny never led the world to peace and harmony. He continued selling ice in the summer and coal in the winter until his sixty-fifth birthday when he retired and got a pension. A few months after his sixty-fifth birthday, he dropped dead of a heart attack. By that time Auntie Rifka was also dead. My cousin Shaindel was put away in a home. My cousin Moe continued the ice and coal business. Bertha got married and became the mother of four children who were normal like the rest of us.

My mother used to tell the story of how Uncle Benny was the Messiah but never knew what to do about it, and the whole family would shake with laughter because she was such a wonderful story-teller. They particularly liked the way she mimicked Uncle Benny trying to imitate God's voice.

But I never found the story funny. I always felt it was too bad for all of us that when Uncle Benny was the Messiah he hadn't known what to do.

Big Boys Shouldn't Cry

I FOLLOWED MY FATHER OUT OF THE HOUSE AND ran after him shouting, "Pa, hey, Pa!" but my father paid no attention. He kept walking and cursing to himself, muttering under his breath, "They're trying to get me."

"Go with him," my mother said. "Don't let him walk around by himself. Try to bring him home."

I reached my father's side and looked up at his face and felt strange. I had fought two of the boys on the street who had called my father "crazy." "It's a nervous breakdown," I screamed at them, "and that's different from crazy."

Now I looked around to see if any of the gang was in sight. The street was empty. There was a little snow on the pavement and it made a sound like dried toast breaking when I walked on it. In the spring, I thought to myself, Pa would be better. It only lasted for a few months. The doctor said maybe three months, maybe six months.

My father was muttering to himself. "They're trying to get me. They're trying to get me."

"No, Pa," I said, "no one's here but me."

"I've got an invention that'll make millions. . . . Fools can't see it. . . ."

"Shh," I said, "shh. . . ." I hated when my father talked foolish like that.

I saw a man coming towards us. "Sure, Pa," I said, laughing. "Gee, that's funny, Pa. That's a swell joke all right." I talked loud when the man passed. The man didn't pay any attention to us.

My father stared at the ground as we walked. "History repeats itself. . . . The glory of the world and the things therein amen. Amen. Amen. Amen. Quietly shadows quietly quietly quietly. Music. My foolish friends. My foolish idiotic imbecilic friends. How little. How *little* little you know. How in the everlasting." He began to giggle.

I bit my lip. "Please let's go home, Pa. Please. . ."

My father started to laugh out loud and then to sing. "Glory. . . glory. . . a man a man oh oh/ Oh the pity the pity/ Oh the pity kitty kitty."

I pulled at his sleeve. "*Papa!* We've got to go home. We've just *got to!*"

My father looked down at me. He smiled, a foolish kind of smile. It made me sick. "Go home, David," he said. "I've got big business to attend to."

"*Pa, please, Pa!* And then people were passing. "That's a good idea, Pa. We'll go to the movies and come home in time for supper. Sure, that's the best thing." But this time the people stared at us.

"Pa," I said quickly, "you know what? Let's go home and we'll make an invention and we'll go on that farm, huh, Pa? Let's go and do it. We'll make an invention and we'll get everything."

My father stopped at a street corner and stared. His lips were curled in disgust. His chin kept falling lower and lower and I stood in front of him, hoping that people wouldn't see my father's face when it got that way. After a long while my father looked up with closed eyes. Then he opened them and looked at me. "Hello, son," he said. He was speaking in his normal voice. It was like it sounded when he told me stories. "What are you doing out of school, David?" he asked gently.

"It's Christmas holidays, Pa. . . ." I grabbed my father's hand happily. We looked at each other, both smiling. He's well again, I thought. He's well again.

"I've been walking along," my father said, "thinking. Oh, I've been thinking about a lot of things. Would you like to walk with me?"

"Sure, Pa. Let's walk home."

My father smiled down proudly at me. "You're a handsome boy, David. You look just like your mother. I've been thinking," he said thoughtfully, trying hard to remember. He looked around him absent-mindedly, as if trying to recall something. He frowned. "Darned, David, if I can remember what I was thinking. . . Simple. . . Simple little things. . ." He looked startled. "Shh," he said to me.

"They're trying to get me!" he said, his face suddenly white.

"Oh, Papa."

For a second my father seemed to know. He seemed to know what was happening and, knowing, he collapsed inside, allowing the fear to seize him, and he realized he was holding me with his two hands, shaking me, and my head was bobbing up and down. He let his hands loose and turned, walking away quickly. A streetcar stopped and he got on. I followed him and paid our fares. I sat beside my father. I smiled, trying to make them think that my father and I were having a good time.

Then he started to talk out loud, fast, one word after the other, and it wasn't the same on the streetcar as on the street, and all the people stared at him.

I laughed. "That sure is funny, Pa. . . . That's a swell story."

My father glared at the people. "Bastards!" he shouted. "What the hell do any of you know? You know what it is, the world, your heads, the dirt. . . You know? You don't know a goddamn! A miserable world with miserable people."

A girl giggled. I said, "It's our stop, Pa. . . . Let's get off. It's our stop. Look." I heard somebody say "drunk," and the people were staring at Pa and spit was running from Pa's mouth and I couldn't stand it any longer. I held my breath and looked down at my feet, but the sobs came out and then it got so that everyone could hear them and I sat there not moving, with my head hunched and trying not to breathe or think or feel.

My father turned and when he saw me crying he stopped talking. He stared at me in surprise. "Davie? Crying? A big boy like you crying? What are you crying for?"

"It's our stop. . . Please let's get off. . . Please let's get off, Pa."

"Sure, Davie, we'll get off. Come tell your father all about it." He took my arm and we got off the streetcar. I couldn't stop crying. "Shh, Davie," my father said, "nothing can be that bad. A big boy like you mustn't cry."

The Beating

I GOT SOME FREE TICKETS FOR A HOCKEY GAME. It was a very important match between Les Canadiens and the Toronto Maple Leafs, the last of the seven games of the play-offs. Mr. Keller had been able to get a fistful of tickets and gave me two as a gift "to take your girl."

By then I had *three* girls — Susan, Sybil and Marie — and I had to decide which. Marie was out because she and I had had a fight. Sybil didn't like hockey all that much. Susan loved it, so the decision was easy.

Now my Uncle Willie gets into the story. He had an extra ticket for the game (also from Mr. Keller) and, as he didn't care much for hockey, he gave it to me. I didn't tell him I already had two.

Uncle Willie's ticket was right next to the ones I had, so I planned to ask my friend Mendel. I made the mistake of boasting to my mother that I had three tickets for a play-off game and she let out a yell, "Take Joel! He loves hockey!"

"It's too late for him!" I protested. "It'll keep him up too late!" The game started at eight-thirty and didn't finish until after ten.

"So he'll oversleep and be late for school once," said my mother.

"Yah! Yah! Yah!" shouted my six-year-old brother.

29

"Take me! Take me! Take me!"

I took him. Unwanted. But I took him. He sat next to us and I instantly forgot his unwelcome presence. This was it, remember. The series was tied three games apiece. Whoever won this game took the Stanley Cup. Our forward line consisted of Howie Morenz, Auriel Joliet and Pete Lepine. That's having three super-stars on your team. The Maple Leafs didn't have a chance. Our players were inspired that night. By the third period we were leading four to two. My God, what a game. What plays, what fights, what narrow misses, what saves, what stick handling, what goal tending, what passing! Susan and I shouted ourselves hoarse with the rest of them.

Need I tell you Les Canadiens won? Five to three. How proud the players were as they skated around the ring following their captain Morenz who held the coveted Stanley Cup high in the air.

Writing a poem or a great play, climbing a mountain never climbed before, falling in love, having a baby, seeing justice done, listening to a great symphony, watching a glorious sunset — what are these experiences compared to the joy of one's team winning the Stanley Cup?

Susan and I skipped home recalling every play. What a game! What a game! This was probably the moment I fell in love with her but didn't know it. I invited her in for tea. We entered the house flushed and excited. My mother looked behind us and asked, "Where's Joel?"

Susan and I also looked behind us. I opened the door and looked. I ran downstairs and looked down the street.

I had lost my kid brother.

I climbed back up the stairs and assured my mother Joel was still sitting in the Forum waiting. We had walked out thinking he was following us.

"How could you not notice he wasn't with you?" my mother shouted.

My father listened silently, then spoke with his new voice of authority: "Go and find him."

Susan and I rushed out of the house and ran all the way. We were frightened and guilty.

"I thought he was walking behind us," I said.

"So did I," said Susan.

The Forum was closed and there was not a sign of Joel. I phoned home. Maybe he'd arrived. My mother was hysterical. A neighbour had seen Joel on a truck heading north.

"He's been kidnapped!" my mother screamed. "My big revolutionary! He's lost his little brother!" She keened and cried.

My father got on the phone. "I've telephoned the police," he said, more authoritative than ever. "You get yourself home right away."

I told Susan it was better if she didn't come home with me. I had to face this alone. By now I was holding back my own tears. I liked my kid brother, even if he was a pest and wanted to go wherever I went. I last remembered him in the seat beside us, shouting his head off. I also remembered that when we got up to go, he did too. I didn't recall seeing him after that.

When I got home, a policeman was taking Joel's description, my mother was sitting on a chair, rocking to and fro, her face bloodless, low, deep moans coming from her. My sister Sarah kept saying Joel probably found some friend and went to his house, but it was now eleven-thirty at night. My mother didn't look at me, but my father kept giving me very funny looks.

"How does a person lose a brother?" my mother kept muttering. Then she'd fix me with a crazy look. *"How does a person lose a brother?"*

I went into my room and prayed. I told God if He brought back my kid brother I would never commit another sin as long as I lived. I promised Joel my ice skates, hockey stick, roller skates, boy-scout knife, live grasshopper — all the things he wanted. He could have everything. Only bring him back.

Then I heard a shriek. When my mother screamed, it was difficult to know if she was happy or tragic. Joel was back. He'd turned up on a truck around midnight, grinning and eating an apple. Mama fainted, but we finally heard what had happened.

Joel had met a classmate, Hershel, whose father had a truck. Hershel had invited him to go to the Laurentians to deliver some fruit. He had called out to Susan and me, but we hadn't heard him.

During all this my father had maintained an unnerving silence. My mother said she was too nervous to sleep, so she went to visit a neighbour.

My brother and sister slept in the same room, and I in a little one off the hallway. When they had fallen asleep, my father opened the door of my room and I saw he was holding a strap in his hand.

"Turn over," he said. "I'm going to teach you a lesson you'll never forget."

I was as tall as he was and probably in better condition. But I thought: He wants to make a point. He hasn't been treated with enough respect around the house. He'll give me a few whacks on the ass to show everybody who's boss.

I turned over in my vest and shorts, and he began to hit me. I counted to three and he hit me again and I figured, okay, one for good luck. But he kept swinging away with all his might and couldn't stop, and I just lay there until he tore through the cotton and my flesh and the bed was soaked in blood.

"Say you're sorry," he kept muttering, but I refused to open my mouth and kept my teeth clenched.

The noise had awakened both Sarah and Joel, and they

ran in, frightened and crying, trying to pull my father away.

Finally, he stopped from exhaustion. On seeing what he had done, he hurried to the phone to call a doctor. When my mother came home and saw me smeared in blood, she fainted again. By then my father was in shock. "I didn't mean to hit him like that. I had a blackout," he said.

The doctor arrived and bandaged me. My mother told him I'd been in a street fight but he knew she was lying.

The moment the doctor left, my mother pounced on my father. "Shouldn't you commit yourself? You almost killed him."

"I had a blackout," he repeated. He came into the room. "I'm sorry. I didn't mean to hurt you like that. I had a blackout."

I stared at him, and his eyes drifted. We both knew that things would never be the same between us again.

A Menace to Society

HIS REAL NAME WAS ABRAHAM BUT WE CALLED him Abe or Abie until we heard his father call him *Schvantz,* and the name stuck. When I asked my mother what it meant, she said, "Louse." Later I discovered it was a Yiddish vulgarism for penis. He accepted the name because he didn't understand its meaning either. He was a few years older than the rest of us on the street. Our average age was ten, so figure his for thirteen or fourteen; and he was a good head taller than any of us.

Our teacher, Miss Evans (Yes, Miss Heavens! No, Miss Heavens!), said she had no doubt he was either mentally backward or emotionally disturbed. Whatever, he was an obsessive pilferer and couldn't stop himself from stealing. Anything. Pens, pencils, odd bits of stationery and books from the teacher's desk, from the school storeroom, from our desks.

Miss Evans was the first person I heard describe him as "a menace to society," which pleased him and made the rest of us envious. A menace to society sounded like a very important thing to be. I kept wishing I was one, but you had to have a special talent for it or be born with it, as Schvantz had.

Miss Evans kept sending him to the principal to be

punished. Schvantz would undertake these journeys from classroom to principal's office with a bit of swagger.

Eventually his mother had to come and speak to the principal, who gave her a stern lecture on the need to discipline her son or he'd be expelled. Her husband had only one method for handling this sort of problem. He beat Schvantz mercilessly with the buckle of his pants belt. When Schvantz came to school next day, his bruised face puffed and discoloured, Miss Evans asked him if he'd been fighting.

"My fadder beat me with his belt buckle," Schvantz reported.

"Surely not on your face!" said the shocked teacher.

"He beat my ass too," Schvantz assured her. This sent the class into a fit of nervous laughter.

It was obvious that Miss Evans felt guilty about it. A quick succession of looks crossed her face, from compassion to anger to frustration. He was the kind of juvenile delinquent teachers describe as hopeless and social workers as incorrigible.

Whether he was mentally backward or emotionally disturbed or both I was never sure, but at the time I thought he was just plain stupid. He'd remove tires from parked cars on our street. None of us moralized about his predilections but we figured he was pretty moronic to steal spare tires from cars parked on his own street. If you're going to do that, you go to a street where you aren't known — that's if you've got a normal brain in your skull, which he obviously didn't have. So he kept getting caught and sent to a reform school somewhere in the Laurentians where he'd undergo more beatings for pilfering the workshops.

It was only much later that I realized his stealing was a way of getting attention, and that was why he'd steal from cars on our street. He *wanted* to be seen and caught and punished. It gave him status. It made him feel important.

He maintained a high position on the street by virtue of his being taller, tougher, able to run faster, and by his reckless stealing. We considered him fearless because he kept on stealing and being sent to reform school where he'd get more beatings. But he also learned more tricks from the other incorrigibles. He started entering homes and shops in the night and proudly displayed his loot before he sold it to contacts he'd made in reform school.

Whenever the urge got him, he'd urinate in the middle of the street. He'd bend his knees, turning from side to side, as if watering flowers. The girls shrieked and their mothers either laughed or threatened to call the police. I don't recall anyone ever doing it. There was an innocence about him that was disarming and most of the adults on the street liked him. Despite his size, he never bullied the younger, smaller kids. He was also good-natured, eager to be helpful carrying heavy packages for our mothers, and sharing whatever fruit or candy he had stolen.

Another habit which gave him status was his ability to ejaculate, a performance none of us was capable of as yet. We'd gather around him in the back lane. He'd take his pecker out and begin masturbating, and we'd have to move fast out of the way to avoid being spattered. Some of the boys tried imitating him, but no matter how hard they tried, nothing happened except their small erections. I tried it in the privacy of my bedroom or bathroom, with similar lack of success.

Eventually what gave him the highest status he ever held with us was the news that his mother had cancer. In a period of a short year she shrank to little more than a skeleton, and Schvantz kept announcing proudly, "My mudder's got cancer," another achievement none of us could match.

One day she was carried out of their house on a stretcher

and put into a waiting ambulance. The event gave him a new feeling of importance. She died a week or so later, and he swaggered as if he were king of the block. He displayed no sign of grief or sadness, just excitement at all the attention he was getting.

When she was brought back in a coffin, we went to our respective houses to bring him an orange or apple or banana or slice of bread and butter. Some primitive rite was being enacted unconsciously without a word having been said about it. We talked in whispers as we watched him sitting in front of his house, his mouth full, chewing, swallowing, his eyes glistening, the fruit and buttered bread piled around him. Then he began blubbering in a delirium of excitement, "My mudder's belly's all swollen! I t'ink she's gonna have a baby!"

He grinned, expecting new respect and admiration. But it had the opposite effect. One of the boys approached the pile of food and retrieved a piece of fruit he'd brought. The rest of us did the same, wanting the gift of food returned. Bewildered by our hostile behaviour, Schvantz kept asking, "Whatsa matter? Whatsa matter?" but no one could have told him because no one would have known how to express it.

He never regained his status. We stopped playing with him and refused to share his loot. He kept to himself, and as he got older his name began appearing in the newspapers as a chronic offender, until he was arrested attempting to rob a grocery store at the point of a gun. He was sentenced to ten years in St. Vincent de Paul Penitentiary.

Pronouncing sentence, the judge repeated what Miss Evans had said, that he was "a menace to society." But I always thought that if Schvantz had had the gift of gab, he might have replied that society had also been a menace to him.

Two Sisters

ONE NIGHT AS I LAY IN BED I OVERHEARD MY mother talking to my Aunt Kate in our kitchen just off my bedroom.

Aunt Kate was ten years older than my mother and had twelve children, all living. My mother was about thirty-five at the time, and had three children, with me the eldest at fourteen, all living.

They were sipping tea and munching cake and cookies when I heard the following exchange:

Mother: Twelve children in this day and age are too many. Six would have been enough. More than enough.

Katie: I love every one of them.

Mother: Even Elmo?

Katie: Of course! Just because Elmo's always getting into trouble doesn't mean I don't love him.

Mother: That's not just simple trouble. He's already been arrested five times for stealing!

Katie: He's just a bit wild. He'll settle down.

Mother: He'll end up in the penitentiary.

Katie: Bite your tongue. He's so handsome. The girls love him.

Mother: The prison guards will also love him.

Katie:	Elmo was once your favourite.
Mother:	When he was ten years old he was cute. At nineteen he's not so cute getting arrested all the time.
Katie:	He'll grow out of it.
Mother:	He's already grown into it.
Katie:	All right. All right. Change the subject.
Mother:	You're not even forty-eight years old and you have twelve children!
Katie:	I can count.
Mother:	A child every two years for over twenty years. That's ridiculous!
Katie:	What can I do? I married a religious man.
Mother:	What's religion got to do with it?
Katie:	He won't use anything and he won't let me use anything. It's against our religion. A man must not spill his seed. That's what it says in the Bible.
Mother:	What do you call what he's doing if not spilling his seed?
Katie:	You're not allowed to waste it. It's all right if you spill your seed inside the woman, but not outside.
Mother:	Let him not be so religious. You're the one who gets pregnant, not him. He could stop coming inside you. If he won't use anything and he won't let you use anything, let him come out before he shoots off.

There was a long pause.

Katie:	He won't do that. It's against the religion.
Mother:	Papa was also very religious. Do you think he didn't spill his seed? Otherwise Mama would have had twenty children! Like this she only had eight.
Katie:	So Joe is more religious than Papa was. What about Harry? Is he religious?

40

Mother:	No. He uses something. And I also use something. How often does Joe do it with you?
Katie:	When we were first married, he'd do it almost every night and on the Sabbath. Now we only do it on the Sabbath.
Mother:	Now *that's* very religious! Only doing it on the Sabbath!
Katie:	Joe says it's holier when you do it on the Sabbath. It's an extra blessing to do it on the Sabbath.
Mother:	No kidding? I didn't know that. How many times does he do it on the Sabbath?
Katie:	Sometimes two, three times.

Another pause. The sound of tea pouring and cups clinking on saucers.

Mother:	How long does he stay inside you?
Katie:	That depends.
Mother:	Usually.
Katie:	About an hour.

A much longer pause this time.

Mother:	An hour?
Katie:	About. Yeah.
Mother:	He stays inside you for a whole hour?
Katie:	Yeah. How long does Harry stay in you?
Mother:	If he stays five minutes it's long.
Katie:	Five minutes? That's not very long!
Mother:	But an hour. A whole hour!
Katie:	Yeah.
Mother:	What does he do for a whole hour?
Katie:	He shtups. What's he supposed to do?
Mother:	He lies on top of you?
Katie:	Where else is he going to lie shtuping me?
Mother:	What do you do with him lying on you for a hour?
Katie:	What do you mean, what do I do? I lie there.

Mother: You lie there for a whole hour while he shtups
         you?
Katie: What am I supposed to do?
Mother: You don't move around? You just *lie* there?
Katie: If I moved around, he'd think I was a whore.

Another long, long pause.

Mother: Doesn't it get boring?
Katie: Sometimes I fall asleep.
Mother: Maybe you should read a book. What would you
like — raisin or sponge cake?
Katie: I like sponge cake.
Mother: Maybe you should eat sponge cake.
Katie: I said I wanted sponge cake.
Mother: I mean when he's shtuping you.

They both laugh and Mama says, "Shh, we'll wake the kids."

Katie: I think I'll try it next time he shtups me. I'll eat
         sponge cake.

Now she is talking with her mouth full of what I deduce is
sponge cake.

Mother: Tell him it's kosher cake, so it's not against his
         religion.
Katie: You're so lucky.
Mother: How am I lucky?
Katie: Harry is so considerate. Only five minutes.

They laugh again.

Mother: One whole hour! My God!

Crazy Joe

I KNEW CRAZY JOE BETTER THAN ANYONE ELSE in the gang. He liked me. I think it was because I used to talk to him sometimes. But he sure was nuts, poor guy, only there was something about him, something about the way he talked, the way everything used to bother him. If you or I felt bad, we wouldn't cry. But Joe did. And we'd always laugh and say to him, "Whatsa matter, Joe? Whatcha crying for now?" and Joe'd answer, "It's for you. I'm crying for you," and we'd laugh all the more and he'd cry all the more.

I used to talk to him. I'd say, "Joe, you shouldn't cry like that. The boys figure you're nuts when you cry like that. You're a man, Joe, and a man shouldn't cry." But he'd always look at me that same sad way, and say, "David, I know the secret of the world. It's love. It's a craving for love and a need for love."

"But you don't have to cry about it, do you, Joe?" I'd say, and he'd answer, "David, I can't help crying."

Once I said to him, "People laugh at you, Joe, when you cry and it makes me feel bad. Even I laugh, Joe. I can't help it."

"It's all right, David," he said. "Laugh if it makes you feel better."

"But it doesn't make me feel better," I told him.

"That's why I like you, David. You're good, and the good people suffer. You'll suffer, David," he used to say. "You'll suffer worse than any of them, and I cry more for you than for them."

Now I know this sounds nutty, but that's what happened when you spoke to Joe. You found yourself talking almost as crazy as him. But there was something about him. I never said this to any of the boys because they would have laughed at me. But sometimes in spite of myself I'd want to hear him talk.

I remember the night I found him sitting alone in the park. I was coming home from work and there was Joe sitting and staring like he was seeing nothing. The wind was blowing his curly hair over his eyes but he didn't pay any attention. He had girl's hands and girl's eyes. Some of the guys said he was queer, but he wasn't queer that way. Not that anyone ever saw him with a girl.

Well, that night in the park Joe saw me and the first thing he said was, "David, tonight is the twelfth of November."

"So it is, Joe," I answered.

"Tonight twenty-two years ago I was born, David."

"Happy birthday, Joe. I didn't know it was your birthday."

"Would you like to talk to me, David? Would you mind sitting here for a while and talking to me?"

I was in a hurry to get home but I said, "Sure, Joe. I like talking to you."

"You're lonely, David," he said. "You must not be so lonely."

"Now there you go again," I said. "I'm not lonely, Joe. Why, tonight the boys and I are going bowling, then after that we're going to get ourselves some girls. You wouldn't call that being lonely, would you, Joe?"

"That's not what you want to do tonight, David," he

said. "Tonight you want to hold the earth in your arms. Tonight you want a woman to kiss the ache in your heart, David, the loneliness, not the flesh of your lips. It's the loneliness in your heart that makes me want to cry for you."

"Now please don't start that again."

The other guys in the gang would never have let him talk so much. But I was sorry for him, even though he said the things he did.

He turned his head around very slowly and looked at me and I felt he wasn't seeing me. "David," he said, "people need to speak to each other because they're lonely, and yet so few people speak to each other."

"Well, lots of people speak to each other, Joe," I said.

"So few, David, so few. Who speaks what is in his heart? Only I, David."

"And people think you're crazy. You've got to control yourself, Joe. People don't do things like that. Not normal people."

"Yes, David."

"You're a good guy," I told him. "I like you, Joe. And I wish you'd stop feeling so bad about everything. It's not such a bad world, Joe."

"Today I met a girl in the park."

"Well, that's news all right. I'll have to tell the gang. Joe has a girl."

"Yes, David." He spoke to me like I was a kid, like I was the crazy one. "Yes, David. . . ." The way a man would say it to a kid.

"The girl I met was lonely," he said.

"Was she pretty, Joe?"

"She was very beautiful."

"What's her name?"

"I don't know."

"Look, Joe," I said, "you're a handsome-looking guy.

Why don't you get yourself a girl? I bet it'd make you feel better about a lot of things."

"A woman should be cried for more than a man."

"Christ, Joe, all your life you're going to cry. You've got to stop it."

"A woman makes my heart bleed. They are so much lonelier than men, David. You must be good to women. They are better than men. They are much better than men, David. And they are lonelier. They are always lonelier."

"Just the ugly ones, Joe."

"The woman I spoke to today was very beautiful, David. She sat just where you are sitting now. I saw her eyes, and I went to her and said, 'Speak to me. You are lonely. Speak to me and you will not be so lonely. I am your friend.'"

"By Christ, you didn't say that? You said that?"

"Yes, David. It would have helped her if she spoke."

"What did she say?"

"She said it was a line she had never heard before."

"It sure is."

"I said to her, 'Can you deny that you are lonely?' And she said no, she could not deny it, and she cried."

"No!"

"Yes, David, she cried. And I said, 'Speak and you will not be so lonely. I am your friend.' When I said that, she got up and ran away. And I have sat here since, and never have I felt the pain I feel now."

"You frightened the poor girl."

He shook his head. "No, David. A man cannot live who knows what I know."

"Aw now, Joe, you've got to stop feeling so bad about everything. When are you going home? I've got to go now."

I got up. "Happy birthday, Joe." I rushed home to eat supper, and then went to meet the gang in the bowling alley.

I didn't tell them everything but I couldn't help telling

them how Joe frightened a girl in the park. I shouldn't
have, I suppose, but I didn't mean any harm. Next day
they all called him names — Romeo Joe! Casanova Joe! . . .
He didn't say a word to me about it, but I felt lousy.

His folks were normal people like you and me. His
father was a pants presser. Joe had a kid sister and a kid
brother, and they were normal too. His brother was
ashamed of him, but his sister wasn't. She'd yell like blue
murder at anyone she heard calling him Crazy Joe. She
worked in a brassiere factory and the boys used to make a
lot of cracks about it but she never paid any attention.
Only when she heard them say something about Joe. She
once turned to the gang on the corner and said, "All your
brains together, the pile of you, wouldn't go into Joe's
little finger."

Maybe one of the troubles with Joe was that he read too
much when he was a kid. He quit school the same time
most of us did but he read too much afterwards. Maybe it
was that. I don't know. He once had a job running messages
for a pants factory just after he quit second-year high,
but he lost it after working a few months and never had
another one. His sister used to give him spending money.
He never smoked or drank so he didn't need very much.
His kid brother kept clear of the neighbourhood and we
hardly ever saw him. We figured because he was ashamed
of Joe. Joe's ma and pa were nice old folks and they never
seemed to bother Joe much. When you have a crazy kid,
I suppose the best thing is to leave him alone.

Well, you probably read all about what happened to Joe
in the papers. But I saw him and talked to him the night it
happened. It was in the same park and I remember most of
what he said. I had a good ear for music when I was in
school and I was good in memory, got ten out of ten, and
I remember almost word for word what Joe used to say.
Sometimes the boys made me repeat it but I didn't after

that night. It's the first time I'm telling it now except for his sister.

Joe was sitting on that same bench. It was very cold. Near the end of January. I told him to go home. His eyes looked wilder than I had ever seen them before. He wanted to talk.

"David, the secret of the world is loneliness," he said.

"Maybe so, Joe, but it's cold as hell. Let's go home."

"Some day it will be love, but now it is loneliness and no one can help it. No one, David."

"Well, then there's no use crying anymore, eh, Joe?"

"No, David," he said, "there is no use crying anymore. Tonight I have stopped crying."

"Well, that's swell, Joe. Now how about you and me going home?"

"That girl came back, David."

"The girl who cried? The girl you frightened?"

"Women are so good, David. They are like flowers, and if given love they bloom and give a fragrance that is sweet and good. But, David, a woman without love is like a flower without earth. It dies, and a woman dies easier than a man."

"What happened?" I asked.

"Her name is Emma, and today she came to me and said, 'I had you wrong.' She had seen my tears and she came to me when she saw my tears and said, 'I had you wrong.' And I said, 'I cry for myself and for all those who are lonely, and all will be lonely until there is love.' And she kissed me. She held my hands and blew her warm breath on them and kissed my cheek and cried with me. . . ."

"What happened?"

"We cried and she left."

"You both cried and she left?"

"Yes, David."

"You found your woman, Joe," I said. "She sounds as crazy as you."

"Poor, lonely David."

"Do you know where she lives?" I asked.

"No."

"Don't you want to know?"

"What difference does it make? Oh, David, you will never see. Never. No one will see."

I tried to make him come home but he sat there like a piece of wood and then said in a whisper, "David, the air is dead tonight."

I left him on the bench in the cold and next day he was found dead. It had snowed during the night and they say his blood was frozen. His throat was cut and his wrists were cut. They found a razor blade beside him.

You probably read all about it in the papers. How his sister screamed at the funeral that he shouldn't be buried, that he wanted to be cremated, and how the gang chipped in and bought him flowers, and how his father threw the flowers into the street because you're not supposed to have flowers at a Jewish funeral. You read that a woman was chased away from the funeral procession, but the papers never told you it was Emma, the diseased whore who had cried with him in the park.

His family moved away from the block a little while later and sometimes the gang would talk about him but they never laughed anymore. They always tried to figure out why Emma Riley came to the funeral, but I never said anything. She disappeared, and for all I know she might be dead too. The way I see it, people like Joe and Emma Riley are better off dead. But who's to judge? It's a crazy world and sometimes I think we're all better off dead, but then I get to thinking maybe I listened too much to Crazy Joe.

Squirrels and Summer Flowers

I WAS MADLY BUT SECRETLY IN LOVE WITH BRINDA Bassell, the most beautiful communist in Montreal. She was eighteen and I was sixteen, but I looked older. She was in love with Peter Tannenbaum, the handsomest communist in Montreal, six feet tall, wavy thick brown hair, a John Barrymore profile, a poet, short story writer, actor and stage director.

It was natural that two of the most outstanding comrades in our city should love each other and just as natural that I, a nobody, glowed and thrived silently in this love. I felt honoured, blessed in their presence every Sunday afternoon at the meeting of our Young Communist League branch. Our little meeting hall, which could seat eighty people at a pinch, was on Esplanade Avenue, facing the fields and hills of Mount Royal, our mountain.

I used to sit unobtrusively at the back, listening to Peter and other leaders of the branch discussing the issues of the day, and to Brinda making intelligent comments or singing during the "social" part of the meeting. Her voice evoked memories of great opera contraltos. Everything about her was extraordinary.

It was good to love her as I did. Keeping it a secret ennobled me to myself. The girl I loved was loved by someone worthy of her. She was happy. So I was happy.

If I suffered a stab of loneliness or sadness, I refused to let myself feel it. To be permitted into Brinda's presence every Sunday separated by only ten rows of chairs was reward beyond my wildest expectations.

At night before going to sleep I'd write love poems which accumulated in secret drawers. Your hair is like a starless night. We are not two, we are one. And so on. Often during the day I'd sneak away from the front of the gift shop where I worked as a clerk and sit in the toilet feverishly writing my verse and prose. This led to unpleasant exchanges with the boss, Mr. Rothenberg.

"Where the hell have you been for the last hour?"

One Sunday afternoon, arriving early as usual for the meeting, I saw Brinda enter without Peter. Afterwards, Morty Breslau, a McGill medical student, told me that Peter had moved to New York. A left-wing theatre group had hired him as resident director.

Did that mean Brinda was also leaving? Morty did not know.

Next Sunday I was sitting there early, waiting. She was there. I watched for signs of sadness. She must miss him terribly.

The following Sunday Morty relayed some gossip. Peter and Brinda had broken up. She must be devastated. I felt terrible. How could he have left her? I prayed they would come together and resume their beautiful love that had enhanced and sanctified me. I sent Peter silent messages to New York. Return! Write to her! Say you didn't mean it!

I always arrived early for the meetings. She came with a different fellow each time. Playing the field to hide her heartbreak.

During this time, Brinda and I hardly exchanged a dozen words, which made a particular incident all the more surprising. The Sunday meeting had finished as usual and a group of us started for one of the hills on the mountain we had named Karl Marx Hill, to continue our discussions in a more informal manner. We were organizing a protest meeting in our neighbourhood, calling for the boycott of Nazi goods and for higher unemployment benefits. On the way across the field, Brinda was walking beside me. I lingered so that other comrades might catch up, and she wouldn't find herself paired off with a nobody. But no matter what opportunity I gave her to extricate herself, she continued walking beside me.

Then I realized she was doing it deliberately, as a practical joke. I started speaking rapidly to a nearby comrade, trying to control the panic spreading through me. Brinda turned and said, "I've been meaning to talk to you. I wish you'd speak more often at meetings. You make more sense than most of us."

I waited bravely for the burst of laughter this was supposed to provoke, ready to return a witticism to show I could take it. I was wondering why she had chosen me to pick on. I had totally misjudged her. She was a sadistic bitch who enjoyed torturing shy, stupid people like myself.

"So many comrades," she went on, "talk for the pleasure of hearing their own voices. It's a joy to listen to somebody say something he's given some thought to."

Why was she doing this to me? I loved her!

When we sat down on the grass, I tried to get as far from her as possible, but there she was, sitting beside me. I could see the others trying to conceal their laughter. Then she asked if she could put her head in my lap because she didn't want to put it on the grass. I stood up, announcing I had to be somewhere, and moved down that hill. I started to run and could not stop myself from crying at the mindless cruelty of it all. Why had she tried to humiliate me in front of the others?

I asked for a leave of absence from the Young Communist League on the grounds that I had to work Sundays for my

Uncle Benny who delivered ice. Morty Breslau suggested I change my branch. I did, but secretly I thought that Brinda Bassell should be expelled from the YCL, which was dedicated to the idea of brotherhood and comradeship.

One evening Morty came to visit and remarked casually that Brinda had been asking about me.

I nodded and let it pass.

"Any message for her?" he asked. "I'll be seeing her Sunday."

"Very funny," I said. "Very funny."

Morty shrugged and let it go at that.

Time passed.

The Spanish Civil War had begun.

The fascists reached the suburbs of Madrid and were stopped by the city workers and the International Brigade.

To be a part of that! I was too young, yet I looked older. Perhaps I could lie my age into it. To be a member of the International Brigade! To be a volunteer in one of the greatest causes in history!

Would I have the courage? I hoped I would. I might be killed. But for what a cause! And I would no longer be a nobody.

One Saturday evening I went to a party to raise money for medical aid to Spain, and just as I walked in I saw Brinda. I immediately turned and walked right out. But I'd been seen by the hostess, Sadie, a Jewish woman of thirty-five married to a French-Canadian sculptor. I had shown her some of my work and she said I was talented, so I put her down as a well-meaning harmless eccentric who smoked cigarettes like Russians do, the lit end held towards herself. She followed me down the stairs to ask where I was going. "You probably don't like crowds," she said, "but there's an editor here I think you should meet."

I didn't want to miss an opportunity so I forced myself back. I tried to keep hidden behind other people, but

Brinda finally saw me. Her face went into a bright "loving friends" smile. She pushed across the room. I waited for the attack, sneering bravely. When she got to me, she didn't know what to say and finally managed "Hello." This wasn't too bad, and I looked down and up and sideways, feeling my eyes rolling. I figured I'd commit myself to a good mental hospital in the morning. Then she said, "It's good to see you! Where have you been? I've missed you."

I looked to see if she was performing for the benefit of an audience but nobody seemed to be paying any attention.

I heard somebody humming and realized it was me.

Then I turned around and walked out of the room again. She followed and stood on the step above me. "What have I done?" she asked. "Why are you behaving like this?"

I studied her carefully. People were pushing past us, going up or down the stairs.

"I don't understand," she said. "Morty Breslau gave me some strange message from you a long time ago. What have I done that you're angry at me? All I know is that I like you and I've fallen over myself showing you. . . And you. . ." she faltered.

There was nobody else on the stairs. I heard someone humming and realized it must be me again.

"I don't know why you'd like me," I said, "especially after somebody like Peter Tannenbaum. . . ."

"That's all over," she said, "long ago. And I. . ."

I interrupted with an impatient wave of my hand. "All I'm trying to say is if you're making fun of me. . ."

Her mouth was open. "Are you sure *you're* not making fun of *me*?"

There were tears in her eyes. "You're a crazy boy," she said. "Let's not go back. Let's go for a walk."

I kept looking behind to see whether a group of her friends would swoop on us, whooping with laughter. I didn't believe any of it, but as we walked I started to let myself believe, to let it enter me slowly, so that I finally asked, "You like me? You *really* like me?"

She bent forward and touched my lips with hers.

I had to sit down. I sat on the curb and she sat beside me.

Then we walked for hours and she told me of her childhood. I told her of mine.

I remember the scent of her hair, the husky whispering quality of her voice, her hand in mine, slightly perspiring, our eyes meeting and holding, and then we were at her doorway, and I bent to kiss her cheek.

I kept myself awake as long as I could, fearing if I slept I'd waken to discover it was a dream.

Next morning I knew everything had changed. I was a new person and the world a new place. I played the radio softly. Mozart helped put me in touch with all the galaxies. I walked to the window, my eyes with the shapes and tints of the flowers on the wallpaper, the fading colours now alive, merging with me. I related to everything: the maple leaves on the tree outside, the blue space of sky and cloud beyond; the full-throated miracle called robin singing its heart out, throbbing with the same blood and energy and also, no doubt, in love; the veins, arteries of a leaf becoming a city of streets, gardens and pathways, molecules of light patterns in my eyes; the intoxicating air of summer morning, heavy with the scents of the mountain and the city; sounds of tramcars, motorcars, people, distant planes and distant stars, all there with me, the mind expanding, the body and mind one, no separateness, all one, merging, earth and sky, universe and beyond, all pulsating and finding thought, feeling and expression through *me*! To be alive! To love and be loved!

My mother's "What's the matter with *you* this morning?" couldn't destroy my mood.

My father was oblivious to everything but his Sunday

paper. As his authority seemed directly proportionate to his earning capacity, and as that had been almost nil for years now, his presence evoked tolerance rather than love or respect. He had become, with the years, more of a guest in the house, a boarder who was behind with his rent. My mother would sometimes forget this and involve him in family matters.

"Take a look at your son," she said. "Something's happened and he won't tell us what."

My father gave me a quick bored look and returned to his newspaper.

Reminded thus of reality, my mother gave her usual shrug and poured him a fresh cup of tea, with a look that combined past love, present nausea and future pain.

I gulped my tea and started to leave, muttering I'd be gone for the day. My mother suddenly declaimed, like someone announcing a birth, "It's a girl!" and ran to block my way. "You've got a girl, right? You're not going to a stupid meeting! You're going to meet a girl, right?" I tried to brush her aside with an impatient gesture. "What's her name?" she yelled after me. "How old is she? Does her father have money?"

Brinda's three pretty sisters and dour-looking widowed father each took the opportunity to pass through the neatly furnished living room where I sat awkward and self-conscious, the girls hardly suppressing their giggles, the father unable to hide his disapproval. What was all that about? Brinda explained that her father disapproved of boys. As for her sisters, they were impressed because I was a "real" writer who'd had things published. Peter Tannenbaum had not been a favourite with them. *He'd* never had anything published.

That afternoon on the mountain amidst the squirrels and summer flowers, I took a jump of a thousand years. I told her how long I had loved her. She told me she loved me. We kissed. If you could call that a kiss. Lips barely touching. Bodies trembling, flying.

There was one small shadow difficult to deal with. Sex. Being intelligent forward-looking Marxists, Brinda and I considered ourselves sexually emancipated. That meant we were able to refer to genital organs and sexual intercourse without embarrassment, and agreed that men and women in love should live together as long as they wanted.

But in practice we both suffered from puritanical attitudes. When Brinda informed me she was still a virgin and wanted to remain one until she was married, I was secretly relieved — and unabashedly accused her of being petty-bourgeoise.

But I got to be less shy with her.

We progressed to necking.

She had more experience than I did, and gently guided me along.

We got to heavy petting. At first this was pleasurable and satisfying, but with time I began expressing irritation over our love-making, suggesting it might be healthier and more Marxist to have intercourse. She expressed doubts and anxiety, still determined to be a virgin for her husband.

I began wondering if she was as intelligent and as great as I had first believed. I found fault with little things she said or did. She licked her upper lip when she was thinking. And, naturally, I found fault with myself for finding fault with her. The magic was wearing off.

And so more time passed, a month, two, three, and I learned to live with the new feelings, as most of us learn to live with everything.

Now the love affair took a strange turn. Brinda's brother-in-law, Eddie Mercer, spoke with a decisiveness I found impressive. He was a presser in a ladies' garment factory where his wife, Lillian, also worked, and I was flattered that he considered me mature enough to spend time with.

He and Lil appeared to be an ideally married couple.

One night, as he and I were coming from a meeting where we'd heard a Spanish republican leader speak, I was shocked when he revealed that he and Lil were discussing a divorce. The marriage wasn't working out and he was planning to leave the city and find work elsewhere.

I asked if he was thinking of joining the International Brigade. No. He felt he was needed in Canada to organize trade unions. He didn't have the temperament to fight in the trenches. He'd have to do his fighting against the class enemy at home. I told him of my secret dream to join the International Brigade and become part of the greatest crusade the world had ever seen.

"Then why don't you volunteer?" Eddie asked.

"I have reasons," I replied mysteriously, unable to tell him I wasn't eighteen yet. I kept my age a secret from everybody. I'd have volunteered for Spain right away if I hadn't had to show my passport. Where else in the world should a young revolutionary poet have been but in Spain?

It was a blistering cold winter night. Sidewalk and street were covered with ice. We made our way struggling and slipping through a freezing wind. Suddenly he asked, "Are you planning to marry Brinda?"

I shrugged and said I didn't know.

"Have you slept with her yet?"

The question embarrassed me. I shook my head.

"Why not?" he persisted.

"She wants to remain a virgin until she gets married," I replied, hoping that would end the conversation.

"Hah!" he muttered, and was silent for a moment. Then he stopped and, giving me a strange piercing look, said, "I happen to know she isn't a virgin."

The unexpectedness of the statement had me speechless. I eventually mumbled that I didn't think it was his affair and I didn't want to hear any more about it.

"You're my friend," he said, "and I think you should know the truth."

"I don't want to hear!" I shouted, pulling away, and slipped, falling heavily. As I went down I held out my left hand and felt my shoulder go. I had first dislocated it when I was fourteen skiing down the mountain side one night imagining I was a bird.

Eddie led me to a nearby hospital as I groaned and gasped. He could not stop talking about Brinda. "I don't want to hear it!" I kept saying, almost fainting, but he was like a drunkard unable to control himself. He said that Brinda had slept with a man before knowing Peter Tannenbaum. Eddie even knew where it had taken place. A boarding house on the Main Street, and the landlady had complained because the sheets had been bloody.

"Why are you telling me this now?" I cried out.

"I started it so I'm finishing it," he said.

A sleepy-eyed hospital intern who luckily knew something about dislocations put my shoulder back into place and I happily passed out. When I came to, my arm was in a sling and the pain gone.

Eddie moved to help me down the hospital steps. I told him I didn't need his help any longer. I didn't understand why he had spilled what he had and I wanted to be alone.

He walked off, and I made my way to an all-night café and had some coffee. It was about one in the morning. I telephoned Brinda. Her father answered, angry because I had awakened the house. I insisted on speaking to her, and the urgency in my voice persuaded him. I told her to meet me and I'd explain when I saw her. She kept asking what was the matter, but all I said was, "Get down here. I have to talk to you."

I ordered another coffee and waited. She came in and sat opposite me, her face pale with cold and fright. I dismissed my sling. That wasn't why I had called.

"Why did you tell me you're a virgin?" I asked. "Why did you lie? What was the point of it?"

She sobbed. The café owner and customers looked uneasy.

"Eddie is the last man you should have confided in," I said.

She could not stop sobbing but she did try to explain. This "thing" had happened a couple of years ago, before she had met Peter. She'd had a crush on a man. He had taken her to this room. It had been a frightening experience. She wanted to forget it. She had managed to do that by convincing herself it never happened.

But why the insistence on not having intercourse until she married?

"I don't know why," she said. "I just had to do it this way."

"Why do you think Eddie told me?" I asked miserably.

"Maybe because he's jealous of you."

"What reason does he have to be jealous of me?"

She shrugged. She wiped her eyes and blew her nose.

I walked her home, not saying anything. I felt that we had both been indecently assaulted and very soon I wasn't allowing myself to feel anything.

It was next day in the store, in the middle of a transaction, that it struck me — one man only could have known all the details of that encounter on Main Street. I walked out of the store without a word, leaving a surprised customer, and an angry boss. I telephoned her from a booth.

"The man was Eddie."

We met in a downtown restaurant and she filled in the rest of the story.

"He married Lil and they moved into the house. I was still in high school. He'd come home early from work. We'd be alone. He took me to this room. It was a nightmare. The landlady wasn't angry only because of the

61

sheets. She came into the room because I was screaming. Eddie is a sadist. He hurt me badly. I was ashamed. I made sure nobody knew. And I never let him touch me again. He used to make the occasional pass, but he stopped — and in time it was forgotten. Lil seemed happy, but I know she's not. He beats her and she's getting a divorce. Don't look like that."

I wasn't aware of how I was looking.

"Please don't look like that. I'm glad it's out in the open and there isn't a lie between us anymore. I love you. Please forgive me."

"I forgive you," I said. "I just wish you hadn't lied, that's all."

"I wish so too," she said. "I'll never lie to you again about anything."

I never gave her the chance to prove it.

I called her less and less, and eventually found the courage to say it would be best for both of us if we didn't see each other. Tearfully, she suggested I might feel differently after a short holiday away from her. I said if I did, I'd call her. I never did.

Birdie

HERE I STAND ON THIS CORNER AND I'M SEVEN-
teen and there was never another one like me in this city.
Shh, shh, baby, don't be a fool, another part of my mind
tells me. Ha-ha, I repeat: There was never another one like
me in this whole wonderful and terrible city. Who can take
a breath and give it words? Who can take a smell and speak
of it as I do? Look, I walk along St. Lawrence Boulevard
smelling the smells of bakery, delicatessen, meat and fish
stores, and I watch the faces and everything draws me and
repels me at the same time.

Go home and lie down on the couch and do it to myself.
Nobody's home now. Ma went with Pa to the doctor's,
Sarah's at school, the place is empty. Pull down the blinds
and get under the covers. No. I don't have to. I can prove I
don't have to. There! I don't go! I remain standing here.
Oh, agony and awful horrors, does anyone realize how
terrible it is to be alive and young and weak and me?

I will walk again but not towards home. I will walk
towards Laurier Street. All right! So you'll end up in
Birdie's house, but don't think of it now.

Expand your chest and breathe deeply and give that
man passing you now a glare that will make him tremble.
Good. He looked frightened. Now give that woman a look.

Outstare her. There. She thinks you're crazy. How wonderful it is for me to be walking along St. Lawrence Boulevard thinking crazy thoughts and making faces as if. . . No. *Now watch that!* Not as if! *Not as if any of that. Pa* is the sick one. You are a poet, a minstrel boy. You alone can defy the world, like a triumphant, powerful and magnificent god. You are not like him, not really, not ever really. He is sick. Now fling him from your thoughts as you would fling filth from your hands. Shh, shh, go home and pull down the blinds and get under the covers.

But see? I continue onwards towards Laurier and, damn it, forget about Birdie now and forget about the house and the pulled-down blinds. You are not going to Birdie's. You just happen to be going in the same direction.

Now there is the church. Steeple. Saints. Stone. Cement. Cross. Shadows.

Rearrange the words. "The sunlight threw its shadows through the trees and they, swaying gently, prayed silently before the cold magnificence of the stone edifice." *My god! That's good!* "High above the street the figures of the apostles beckoned with the shadows, nodding benedictions and, from inside, the faint but growing strains of an organ gripped me with hands of mighty music." *God! That's really good!* "Slowly envelope me, dear shadows and sunlight, and kiss my thoughts as they kiss you now, here, on this street corner. What am I but a bit of life breathing, existing, throbbing, living, part of a shadow and part of the sunlight, aching, aching to. . ."

"Hya, Davie!"

I turn as if slapped. It's Milty.

"You must be dreaming of making a million. You shoulda seen your face." Milty grins. "Where you headed for?"

I look back at the church, the shadows, the sunlight and the apostles.

"Which way you going?"

"I was going home," Milty says.

"I'm going the other way."

"Okay. Be seein' yuh." Milty waves good-bye.

Damn him. Damn that philistine, oh damn him, damn him!

"Part of a shadow and part of the sunlight, aching, aching. . ."

Damn him!

I stand here alone. I am alone. I will look back at this moment years from now, many years from now, and remember standing here alone, magnificent. I had almost become one with the shadows and the sunlight. Oh, David, sweet David!

I laugh at myself and feel self-conscious, looking around to see if anyone notices. People pass without being aware of me.

There is much to be sad about. That is another good thought to begin with.

Ah, that Packard over there. A woman in it. I cannot see her face but she's young and beautiful. She'll stop when she sees me because when she sees me she'll have to stop.

How wonderful that we should have met like this, and yet it is no surprise. I knew it would happen one day but I did not know how soon. We'll not speak of love for what we have now is a love no two human beings on this earth have ever had before. Sweet love that I at last should find you here this way.

The bathos and hypnotic rhythms leave me and I know that the Packard has long turned the corner but I still try to intoxicate myself with words and thoughts as I reel towards Birdie's house and become instantly sober when I reach her door.

This is Birdie's house, on the second floor, door painted brown, yellow curtains, black doorbell.

Sound of her feet in slippers. The door opens. She stands

there. Smiling. "Hello, David!" The voice is too thin. The face is too fat. I do not like her. Why do I come to see her?

"Hello, Birdie. Feel like going for a walk?"

"Come in."

She is alone. Had she not been alone, she would have said yes to my invitation. The game will soon begin.

"How have you been, David?"

"Oh, fine. You?"

"Swell. I've been reading."

It starts. The game starts.

"You have? What?"

"Shelley. Keats. Would you like to read out loud this evening?"

"Parents gone to a movie?"

"I think so. They'll be late."

"Sure, I'd like to read out loud tonight, Birdie."

She sits down on the sofa under the fringed floor lamp and pats the pillow for me to sit beside her.

"Shall I read first?" her thin voice squeaks.

"Whichever way you prefer." I do not like her and I do not like doing this anymore. Why do I keep coming here?

She starts to read. "My heart aches and a drowsy numbness pains my senses. . . ."

As she reads, I slowly move my hand up her thigh. She makes no sign that I'm touching her. This is the way we read aloud to each other. This is Birdie's game. The piping voice peeps on and my fingers play with her and I think again, So help me God, she's crazier than I am. Why do I keep doing this with her?

"Christ, do we have to go through this damned business of making as if we're reading to each other?"

She looks startled. "David. You promised." She bites her lips nervously, and the look on her face suddenly seems moronic.

"Okay, okay. Keep reading."

66

She reads more quickly now, her breath coming in shorter gasps, and to the very end the words on the page are uttered, heaved out, and then she lies back and closes her eyes. A moment's rest and then, "You read now, David."

"I don't feel like Shelley tonight," I say, grinning inwardly. "Tonight I'd like to read something from Jean Christophe."

"I'd love to hear you read aloud from Jean Christophe," she says, her face serious, no hint of a smile.

I reach for the book and open it somewhere in the middle. "Olivier, on his part, used to write to Christophe's mother without letting him know. . . ." And Birdie listens with a look of complete concentration, as if she was absorbing every word, and her hand slides up my thigh. I drone on, skipping words, skipping paragraphs, but the look on her face never changes, and then it is shudderingly over and I'm disgusted with her and myself.

This is the worst moment. How to get away from her.

"Would you like some tea?" she asks.

"No. I just remembered, I promised my mother to be home early."

"Come again soon," she says.

"Yes, I will. Good-bye now. . ."

"Good-bye. . ."

We never kiss. She takes me to the door and smiles a sweet, innocent smile as I wave to her.

I make my way to the tramway waiting room on the corner and sit on a bench inside. I vow, as I have many times before, never to see her again, never to play this disgusting game again.

Then I start down the street, down Park Avenue with its strange stores and strange faces, the corner of Laurier and St. Lawrence forgotten, the church forgotten, the special thing I am forgotten. I feel very ordinary when I leave

Birdie's house and walk on Park Avenue. Somehow on Park Avenue I can never evoke the thoughts that come to me on St. Lawrence Boulevard.

I try the words again but they are unable to conjure up the old magic. Slowly envelope me, dear shadows and sunlight. Words. *Words!* And anyway, there's no more sunlight. It's dark now and *these* shadows have nothing to do with me.

I hurry along Mount Royal, back towards St. Lawrence, my pace quickening until I burst into a furious run and don't stop until I reach the corner of St. Lawrence. I lean against the corner ice-cream parlour, my breath heaving. I don't look back now but start slowly, forcing myself to walk leisurely, smiling, feeling my heart quicken, feeling the thoughts coming, the words forming.

Oh, great God in heaven, it's happening again! I'm here again and at one with everything and magnificent again. Flickering store lights and night flies, sad faces passing me on the street, Montreal, city, stone, bricks, wood and garbage cans, aching winds and joyful heavens, odours of fish and fruit and meat and clothing stores. You girl there and you boy there and you old man and old woman there, *look at me!* I'm your singer and your song, your minstrel boy! Oh, stay with me, stay with me, stay with me forever and never let me go to Birdie's again.

Hester, the Whore

MY MOTHER WAS THE YOUNGEST OF SIX CHILDREN. She had a sister and four brothers, the youngest of whom lived with us from time to time. His name was Willie and he and my mother were close.

When I was about five, Uncle Willie lived in a room in our house and paid my mother rent. The street we lived on was called Cadieux, but later it was changed to De Bullion because Cadieux Street had become notorious as Montreal's red-light district. We lived a few blocks south of the infamous neighbourhood, but whenever we mentioned the name, people would snicker.

My Uncle Willie was handsome and cheerful. In winter he wore spats and in summer he wore gaily coloured shirts. He always seemed to have more money on him than any other member of the family. Every Sunday he'd flip coins into the air for me to catch. If I caught one, he'd flip another, higher and higher until I'd miss. I saved this money in a small bank, dreaming of the day I'd have enough to buy a two-wheel bicycle.

In time we moved out of that neighbourhood and Uncle Willie married a pretty girl called Hester. I was secretly in love with her. I think all my cousins were as well. She had long, shapely legs she enjoyed showing off, and she always displayed the upper parts of her creamy-skinned breasts.

For reasons I did not understand, my mother began referring to her as "Hester, the Whore." This saddened me because it meant we no longer visited Aunt Hester's house and she no longer visited us.

When I was about eleven, Uncle Willie came back to live with us. By then Aunt Hester had given birth to a daughter. "She doesn't even look like Willie," my mother said.

As I grew older I was let into the family scandal. My Aunt Hester kept getting caught in bed with strange men. "You'd think," my mother observed, "she'd have brains enough not to get caught." But brains was one quality my Aunt Hester lacked. Pretty face, pretty legs, luscious breasts, but not too much brain. That still did not prevent me from finding her delectable.

As the years passed, Uncle Willie lost his cheerful disposition, and eventually he and Aunt Hester were divorced. By then she'd had another child, a boy this time. Both children moved in with their father and lived with us. My mother brought them up. Uncle Willie paid rent and extra for food.

Uncle Willie made a good living by dealing cards in gambling establishments. I do not recall a time he was ever out of work or out of funds. He was devoted to his children, whom my mother cruelly said were not his, but she never repeated this in front of them. Why she said such things I don't know, for she never displayed anything but warmth and affection for them.

Uncle Willie got older and his eyes went bad so he had to stop dealing cards for a living. To make matters worse, he developed diabetes and heart disease. My mother continued to take care of him until she herself developed diabetes and heart disease, a family curse. Because of this, Uncle Willie had to go live in the Old Peoples' Home. This was a destiny everyone in the family hated and feared.

In the meantime, my cousins married, but neither wanted Uncle Willie to live with them. It was just as well he was in that Home because he'd become very weak and needed constant nursing. At times he'd get up enough energy to come visit my mother. They would sit for hours saying very little, and then he'd take the streetcar back to the Home. On the occasions I did see him, I couldn't help remembering the cheerful, vigorous man of my childhood and the way he had flipped coins into the air for me to catch.

I had arrived one morning from England where I was living, the very morning Uncle Willie had come to beg my mother to let him move in with her and my father. But she refused. "I'm too sick, Willie," she told him. "You need someone to feed you. I'm too sick to cook."

"I'll cook for myself," Uncle Willie pleaded. "I don't want to go back to that place. I don't want to die there."

It was clear he felt he was dying and wanted to be with his family, but my mother was ill in bed and my father was helpless with Parkinson's disease. So my mother insisted that Willie return to the Home. I offered to drive him but he refused.

Later that same day I was driving and I saw my Uncle Willie hurrying along the sidewalk, gasping for breath, his face blue-grey as if with cold, despite it being a hot summer day.

I stopped and asked him where he was running. He could barely speak, he was so out of breath. But he managed to tell me he had called on all of his brothers, asking them to let him live with them until he died, but each had refused and insisted he go to a hospital. I told him I'd take him there.

"I don't want to die in a hospital or in that Home," he said, looking terrified.

I offered to get him a hotel room.

"No," he gasped. "I don't want to be alone in a hotel room. I'm going to try my sister Miriam. Then I'll try my children."

"Why don't you try your children first?"

He started sobbing. I'd never seen an old man cry before. I helped him into the car and drove him to his daughter's house. She said she didn't have room for him, but she telephoned her mother, who asked to speak to him.

Uncle Willie listened to his ex-wife without saying anything, nodded without speaking, then replaced the receiver and sat down. By now his face was the colour of ashes. "She says I can stay with her," he said, his eyes staring blindly.

That evening I told my mother that Hester, the Whore, had taken Willie into her house. It was one of the few times in her life that my mother had nothing to say.

One for the Little Boy

We walked along the rain-splattered highway and my father kept complaining that we'd both catch pneumonia. Finally, to placate him, I said, "It's warm rain. It's like having a warm shower."

"Warm shower?" he repeated. "Warm sponge bath you mean. It's sticky. I don't like feeling sticky."

I noticed the similarity of our gait, the way each of us stepped on the ball of his foot and bounced forward. We both had a habit of hunching our shoulders as if our clothes were slipping. Pa wore a raincoat; I, a leather jacket, and I carried a knapsack on my back. Both our caps were soaked tight to our heads.

I stopped to adjust the knapsack and studied the broad shoulders of my father walking in front of me. He was broader but shorter than I was. His shoulders were reminders of a body that had once been healthy and powerful. When I came up alongside of him and looked at his face, the momentary illusion his broad shoulders had created disappeared. His face was sallow, sickly, unshaven, and his black, brooding eyes looked blacker and sadder for it.

"Let's stop now and find a place to sleep," he grumbled. "You can take it," he added, appraising me. "You're a young buck of eighteen. I'm approaching fifty, did you forget?"

"No, but we're in a spot. I told them I'd be there for the job yesterday. I'm a day late." I threw my hands out in an exaggerated shrug and tried to make light of it. "It's one of those things. We have to keep going. It can't be helped."

"Bah," he said in disgust. "Bah! Bah!"

"Black sheep," I grinned.

He shared my grin quickly. "We used to have good times, didn't we?"

I nodded. We kept closer together now as we walked and the wind grew stronger.

"Say," he said, touching my arm, "did you ever hear my Italian accent? Listen. Mussolini hadda lotta da hair on his chest, but dey hanga him by da hair onda heels. Not bad, eh?"

I shrugged. Not good either, but I didn't say anything.

"Listen to this one," he said, coughing to clear his throat. "The rain is my wife. It spoils my life. A woman is hell. Her tongue is a bell. Right on the spur of the moment they come to me like that. Not bad, eh?"

I nodded grudgingly.

"Aw shut up!" my father shouted angrily. "Always sticking up for her! *Shut up!*" He began muttering to himself. "We'd have been on easy street if it hadn't been for her. *Women!*" His voice was heavy with disgust.

"Pop," I said, "we're going to need new shoes."

"Yes, we'll have to get new shoes. My feet hurt. You shouldn't have let me walk so far. I have sore feet and I'm not well."

"It's just a little way more. It won't be long now."

The headlights of an oncoming car made the trees on the side dance in the shadows. The hum of the engine and the swish of the tires grew louder. The lights were blinding. The car swept by us and darkness snapped over us again and then it was silent except for the wind, the rain and the sound of our wet shoes.

Pa heaved a sigh. "Not a friendly face. Not one friendly face on this whole trip."

"The truck driver was a nice guy," I said.

He turned in surprise. "He threw us out, didn't he? He threw us out! In the rain!"

I kept quiet.

"He cursed me!" Pa shouted, jabbing his fist at his thigh.

"He didn't say a word. Why do you imagine everybody's cursing you? The truck driver didn't say a word. He was just whistling."

He pulled at my sleeve in a frantic gesture. "You fool," he cried, as if he was about to weep. "That truck-driving bastard was cursing *both* of us!"

He brought his head close to my ear and his voice broke to a hoarse whisper. "He was going to kill us." Pa's face changed to a look of cunning triumph. "That's why I yelled at him. So he'd know we weren't afraid of him. I let him know what he'd have to deal with." Pa's hands were shaking with excitement. He kept pulling at my arm as he spoke. "You don't understand these things!"

I pulled my arm away and walked ahead of him. He kept shouting after me in a high, piercing voice. "Shut up! I know what I'm doing! If it wasn't for me we'd both be dead now."

"You imagined it," I said, tired and fed up and unable to stop myself. "You keep imagining things."

"You're just like your damned mother!" he screamed. "I'm not going with you a step further!"

He stopped at the side of the highway, withdrawing into silence. I trudged back and held my hand out. "Pa," I said.

"Now shut up!" he cried bitterly. "Shut up, damn you!"

"Pa, you're going to be all right, aren't you? You're going to be all right!"

He stared at me. "Why don't you listen to me? You never listen to me."

"I will," I said. "Come on."

"Listen to me," he said as he walked beside me. "Learn to listen to me."

My head was aching from it all. He'd been in a hospital and had left without permission, refusing to go back. My mother had had a heart attack and my sister, Sarah, was taking care of her. I couldn't leave him behind with them. The stress of it would have killed my mother, so here he was with me and my head was splitting from it.

The garage was in darkness when we arrived. It was a small service station just off the main highway. A wooden cottage belonging to the owner, Tom Jenkinson, stood on the right, also in darkness. The night had become cold and we shivered with the dampness. The rain had spent itself. The torrent was over.

"Go wake up the idiots and tell them we're here," Pa grumbled through chattering teeth, glaring up at the black sky, blinking as the dying drops of rain fell into his eyes. "I hate the dark."

I tried the door of the men's room and pushed it open. I dropped my knapsack and took off my soaking cap. "We'll sleep here tonight. Okay?"

"Don't we get a room?" he shouted, throwing his wet cap to the floor. "What the hell kind of place is this anyway?"

"Shh," I cautioned, "you'll wake up everybody. It's almost three o'clock." Then before he could say anything, "They don't know you're with me. They're giving me the job with a room to sleep in. I don't want to wake them up in the middle of the night. It'll be better in the morning." I squeezed his arm in a friendly gesture. "Okay?"

He studied me. "Don't they know I taught you everything you know about cars?"

"Sure, Pa, they know."

"Don't they know you'll need me around when you can't figure something out?"

"Sure, Pa, they know that. Now let's get some sleep. We better get into something dry."

My father removed his raincoat. "At three o'clock in the morning I don't go to sleep," he announced. "You know I always wake up around four. What's the sense of going to sleep for one lousy hour? I bet you the guy who owns this piss-ass station is a lousy mechanic. We'll have to teach him a few things."

"Now look, Pa," I began, but I was too exhausted to continue. "Sleep the hour. You're tired. Get to sleep." I couldn't stop the anger in my voice.

"Remember who you're talking to," Pa said, trying to sound threatening and authoritative.

I gritted my teeth and began pulling things out of the knapsack. I was looking for my flashlight. I found it and focussed on the wall. "We'll have enough room if we sit and sleep against the wall."

"Where did you get the flashlight?" Pa asked.

"Pretty nice, eh?" I played its beam over the walls, then flashed it through the open doorway. The rain had stopped.

"What did it cost you?" His eyes followed the white streak that lost itself in the darkness.

"I got it for a very good price," I chuckled. "Nothing."

He watched me now with half-closed eyes and rubbed his chin thoughtfully. "You stole it?" he asked quietly.

"Let's say I gave myself a gift."

My father stood in front of me. I held the light on his chest, illuminating his shoulders and face.

"I'm asking you if you stole it." His face had a comic fierceness.

"Okay, I stole it."

"I don't like my son stealing." He started unbuckling his belt. "I don't like my boy being a thief. I'm going to have to punish you."

I started to snicker and raised my hand to push him

away, but as I watched the intense, pathetic face of my father raising the belt to strike me, I switched off the flashlight and let my hand drop. The first swing was across my shoulders, making a sharp, cracking sound on my wet leather jacket. I held my head down, waiting and listening to my father's laboured breathing as he kept swinging the belt in short, jerky movements, missing me half the time and panting with each swing. "Let this be a lesson to you."

I remembered another beating once, and he hadn't missed then.

Exhausted, he stood in front of me, his feet astride. "Will you do it again?"

"No."

He slumped to the floor, leaning his head against the wall in weariness. "You never listen to me," he said mournfully. Within seconds he was in a deep sleep.

I took dry clothes out of the knapsack then carefully removed my father's jacket and shirt. Slowly, without waking him, I dressed him in dry clothes. Then I changed my own clothes and sat down beside him. I stared at him through the darkness, trying to make out his features, remembering how he had once looked, how he had once been. I inched closer. I closed my eyes and let my head fall to my father's shoulder, and after a while I fell asleep.

I dreamed it was sunny, bright and warm. The man who owned the garage, Tom Jenkinson, was big and smiling and holding his hand out. My father shook it and smiled his charming smile. My father was well dressed, neat. I was proud of him.

"I'm David's father," he said.

"What luck," said Jenkinson, laughing. "I need a partner. I hear you're an expert mechanic, Mr. Webber. You're an answer to a prayer. Will you be my partner?"

"Of course," my father replied and patted my head. "David's going back to college. He thought *he* was going to work here."

Mr. Jenkinson laughed again. It felt good seeing and hearing him laugh like that. "That's a hot one," he said. "A boy his age should be in college."

"He wants to be an engineer," Pa said and smiled at me. Then he bent forward and took my face in his hands and kissed my cheek like he used to when I was a little boy.

"Bah, bah, black sheep," said Mr. Jenkinson.

"Oh, you know that one too?" I said.

Mr. Jenkinson stopped smiling. I felt a sharp pain pierce me. "Oh, please don't stop smiling, Mr. Jenkinson," I pleaded.

"Who are you trying to kid?" Mr. Jenkinson asked. "Didn't I see you steal a flashlight from my store?" He raised his hand to strike me and my father jumped between us and picked up Mr. Jenkinson as if he were a rag doll. They both started laughing. Mr. Jenkinson said, "I was only joking."

"That's better," said my father. "Now let's get to work. Davie, go to school."

My mother walked into the service station wearing an apron and knitting something. I couldn't tell if it was a sweater or a scarf. She kept knitting but there was no wool on the needles and nothing was happening. It wasn't a scarf. It was something for a baby.

"One for the little boy who lives in the lane," Ma said, smiling.

"Have you no wool?" I asked.

"She doesn't need wool," my father said. "She's dead."

"Should we tell her she's dead?" I asked. "I don't like telling her. She'll feel hurt. Let her think she's alive. She looks happy. Why should we tell her she's dead and make her unhappy?"

"Come, Davie, and eat your supper," my mother said. "Are you happy?"

I loved when my mother smiled. She was so beautiful and had white teeth and flashing eyes and jet-black hair.

"Oh yes, I'm very happy, and Pa is all better. He's become Mr. Jenkinson's partner. He's making good money. I can go back to school."

"That's good," Ma said. "Do you still have bad dreams and wake up at night?"

"Sometimes."

My mother kissed me. Her lips were warm. "Shall I sing you a song like I used to?" she asked.

She's dead, I thought, or else she'd realize how silly it was to sing me a song in the daytime.

"Davie, I know," she said, gazing at me with a perplexed look.

"You know what?" I was afraid to think what she knew.

"I know," she said again in a whisper.

"But it doesn't matter," I said. "Really, it doesn't. If you can come and go like this and be with us, it doesn't really matter if you are."

"It's not good to know you're dead," she said.

My father appeared. He had been away for a long trip. He took my mother in his arms and kissed her. "I love you, Annie," he said. "You know that."

"I love you too," she said.

"It can be the same as always," I said, "if you can come and go like this."

My parents smiled sadly at me. "He doesn't understand," my mother said.

Oh God, I do, I thought. I do. Everything. But I don't want to.

Suddenly I was holding my mother in my arms and staring at my father. He got on my back and played piggyback.

"Do you take good care of your father?" my mother asked.

"Yes, Mother, I do. But he's too heavy. I wish he'd get off my back."

My father climbed off my back and began to cry. I was

afraid Mr. Jenkinson would see him crying. Then Mr. Jenkinson came and said, "Oh, oh, I see your boy is a cry-baby." I had to laugh. Mr. Jenkinson had mistaken me for my father.

"That's because he has to go to school," I said, feeling proud that I could be mistaken for my father. "Now go to school," I said to my father, "and be a man."

My mother put her lips close to my ear. "Take care of him, David."

"Are you going now?" I asked her.

Her face changed colour. I knew she was going. She didn't speak. My father was still crying. Mr. Jenkinson's face became transformed into a tiger's face and his eyes narrowed.

I took my father's hand and led him behind the service station and took his face in my hands and kissed him. Then I hit my father on the temple, not too hard because I didn't want to hurt him. There was scarcely a bruise as my father fell down dead. I wept. "I had to do it," I sobbed. "It was the only way."

I dug a grave. Mr. Jenkinson helped me. We lowered my father's body into the grave. There was a mattress at the bottom so it would be comfortable for him. Then my mother got into the grave and lay beside my father.

"He'll come back just like your mother does," Mr. Jenkinson said.

"I should have done this a long time ago," I said, looking into the grave.

My mother nodded to me. "You should have, yes," she said.

I awoke from the dream in a fevered sweat. It was still dark. My father moaned in his sleep.

I sat there, shivering and thinking, got up and walked out of the men's room, tiptoeing so as not to wake him. I encircled the service station. A pick and shovel were leaning against the back wall. I picked them up and walked to the centre of the field, soft and muddy from the night's heavy rain. I knew exactly what I was going to do. In less than an hour I had dug a deep grave in the wet earth.

I returned to my father and shook him awake.

"What? What is it?" he grunted.

I played my flashlight on his face, making him blink. "Put that damned thing off. What is it?"

"I want to show you something," I whispered.

"What?"

"Get up. I'll show you." I helped him to his feet.

"Where in goddamned hell. . ."

I kept my voice calm and low. "You'll see in a minute."

I held his hand, leading him across the muddy field, and stood before the open grave. I bent down to lift the pick.

"I've got to do it," I said, tears starting to burn my eyes. "It's the only way."

I felt sick at the sound of his skull cracking. I pushed his dead body into the grave with my foot and refilled the grave, making sure there was no telltale mound. I retraced my steps, shovelling mud over my father's footprints, and staggered into the men's room where I sprawled and cried myself to sleep.

The morning light blinded my eyes. "Wake up!" I heard my father saying.

I blinked up at him.

"It was a dream!"

"You dreamed?" my father said. He stared up at the grey morning sky. "Maybe this is also a dream. How can anybody be sure? Let's go wake up the idiots and get some breakfast."

We walked towards the cottage. "Remember," my father said, "let me do the talking."

My Father, the Capitalist

MY FATHER CAME INTO SOME MONEY. HE GOT HIT by a streetcar.

It happened one Sunday morning as he was crossing the corner of Park Avenue and Mt. Royal during a sudden downpour. A passing samaritan helped him get home. When he limped in through the front door, blood dripping from his right trouser leg, my mother screamed and rushed to call Dr. Saperber, the family physician who charged one dollar a visit.

"My husband," she told him, "was just hit by a streetcar."

"Is he dead?" asked the doctor.

"No. He's bleeding and limping," my mother said.

The doctor had a few other emergencies and suggested that my father be brought to the emergency department of the Royal Victoria Hospital, which was closest to us. He said he'd get over as soon as possible.

"It's only a scratch," my father insisted. "I don't have to go to a hospital."

Uncle Willie was living with us at the time — as he always did when he caught his wife, Hester, in bed with another man.

"He's caught her with four different men," my mother said, "so figure how many he hasn't caught her with."

Invariably, Uncle Willie and Hester would reconcile, "for the kids' sake."

Uncle Willie examined my father's leg. The trouser was bloodied, but the wound had stopped bleeding and there didn't seem to be any fracture.

"It wasn't the driver's fault," my father kept saying. "The streetcar skidded."

"Did you take the names of any witnesses?" Uncle Willie asked. "Did you get the number of the streetcar? The name of the driver?"

Of course my father had done none of these things. All he wanted to do was get into bed and lie down.

Uncle Willie phoned the tramway company and reported the accident, urging my parents to hire a lawyer he knew called Louis Baxter.

"Put it in Louis Baxter's hands," Uncle Willie kept nagging. "He'll sue and they'll settle out of court."

My mother was all for doing this, but my father did not like Louis Baxter. "When I asked him to sue that company for stealing one of my ideas, he refused," he said.

My father often accused various companies in the city of having stolen his ideas when they manufactured an item he had mentioned or happened to be inventing at the time.

"This case he'll win," Uncle Willie promised.

"Baxter is a crook," my father said.

"That's right," agreed Uncle Willie. "That's exactly what we need. He has good connections. He'll get you maybe five thousand dollars."

"Let's get this lawyer," my mother said when she heard the amount.

"You say a claims man is coming to talk to me," my father said. "Let's see what he offers."

"You have a chance to make six, seven thousand dollars," Uncle Willie said as he thought of it.

"Eight," added my mother, getting into the spirit of it.

"Eight! Yeah!" shouted Uncle Willie. "Nine thousand dollars maybe!"

But my father insisted on waiting for Mr. Hubbard from the tramway company, who would be calling any day.

One evening after I came home from work, Mr. Hubbard was sitting in the kitchen. Everything about him was thin — his tie, his body, his nose, even his eyes and moustache. Only his clothes had weight: a heavy tweed suit two sizes too large, indicating he might have had more substance at an earlier age. He wore a perpetually thin smile which did not inspire confidence.

From his manner and appearance, I deduced he was related to the president of the tramway company; otherwise, he would not have had such a responsible job.

My mother offered him tea. He accepted and asked how my father was getting on.

"He's limping," she said. "Have you come to look at his leg?"

"No," said Mr. Hubbard. "We have the medical report. We're glad the injury wasn't serious."

"He's limping!" repeated my mother. "That isn't serious?"

"I suppose the pain must have been considerable," said Mr. Hubbard, "but he should be on his feet in a day or two."

"In a few months, years maybe!" said my mother.

I was about to leave the kitchen but my mother ordered me to stay.

"I think," said Mr. Hubbard, "your mother wants you here as a witness, although that isn't necessary."

"He's my son. I want him to stay here. Do you mind?" my mother remarked tartly.

"I don't mind at all," said Mr. Hubbard.

"You've come about the claim." I got into the act. "What's the company offering?"

"A fair settlement," said Mr. Hubbard. "But I think I should see Mr. Webber."

"He's asleep," my mother said.

"I'm awake," came my father's voice.

"He's awake," my mother had to agree, looking sour.

My father walked in with a slight limp.

"This is Mr. Hubbard," my mother said, "from the claims department. . . ."

"I heard," my father grunted.

They shook hands and exchanged meaningless pleasantries.

"That must have been painful." Mr. Hubbard indicated Papa's leg.

"Painful?" my mother scoffed. "Look how he's walking! He may be crippled for life!"

"I won't be crippled for life," my father protested.

"How do you know?" shouted my mother. "Maybe an infection will develop."

"I think," my father sighed, "that she's sorry I didn't lose my leg."

Mr. Hubbard chuckled and relaxed. He knew there was not going to be trouble in this case. "Well, I'm relieved to see you're being intelligent about this matter, Mr. Webber."

"Intelligent?" My mother looked as if she was about to be sick. "That's intelligent?"

"The company," said the increasingly confident claims man, "is prepared to make a fair offer to compensate for the pain, the loss of work, etcetera."

"A fair offer is all we want to hear," said my mother.

Mr. Hubbard took a deep breath. "Inasmuch as it was no one's fault that it had rained that day and the streetcar rails were wet and slippery, inasmuch as it was not a question of the tram driver's negligence, and no question of a mechanical fault with the tramcar, there really isn't very much of a case. I am authorized to offer you one hundred dollars compensation."

86

"What did he say?" asked my mother.

"One hundred dollars," Mr. Hubbard repeated, "plus, of course, the doctor's bills. We'll pay for that."

"Get back into bed!" my mother ordered my father.

"Now, Annie," my father said, embarrassed.

"Get back into bed!" she repeated and turned to Mr. Hubbard. "And you look here, Mister! Inasmuch as it may not be anybody's fault, it was not my husband who skidded into your streetcar but the other way around! And the fact is he won't be able to work for months inasmuch as he can't walk!"

"We understand," said Mr. Hubbard, "that Mr. Webber had been unemployed for some time prior to the accident."

"That gives your company the right to hit him with a streetcar because he's not working?" asked my mother.

"We believe our offer to be a fair one," said Mr. Hubbard.

"Is crippling a man for life fair?" demanded my mother.

"I'm not going to be crippled for life!" My father's voice was getting louder.

"If you told my husband in his present state of mind that there was a dent where the streetcar hit him and you expected him to pay to get it fixed, he'd consider that a fair offer, so don't ask him anything!"

"Enough, Annie," my father said. "I'll think it over, Mr. Hubbard."

"Certainly, Mr. Webber," the tramway man agreed with great respect.

My father limped back to his bedroom.

"Well. . ." Mr. Hubbard smiled at my mother. "We made you an offer."

"And we don't accept it!"

"Do as you see fit," he added courteously. "I don't want to influence you in any way."

"Not much."

"I'll leave my card. If you change your mind, you can phone me."

"If you change your offer, you can phone me," my mother replied.

Mr. Hubbard was at the door. "Good-bye, Mrs. Webber, Mr. Webber. . . ." He turned to me. "I hope your father will be on his feet soon."

"With crutches he'll be on his feet," cried my mother.

Mr. Hubbard slipped out and Mama went berserk shouting and throwing chairs. "A hundred lousy dollars! And he was going to take it! Why didn't you do a dance for him?"

My father limped into the kitchen again, followed by Uncle Willie.

"I have thought it over," he said. "I'll settle for two hundred dollars."

"If they're offering a hundred," Uncle Willie argued, "that means they're expecting to pay ten times that. Leave it in the hands of a lawyer. If you don't like Louis Baxter, hire someone else."

"They've got a medical report," my father said. "They know it wasn't fractured."

"Slip a doctor ten, fifteen dollars, he'll fracture it for you," said Uncle Willie.

But nothing could divert my father from his decision.

"He's doing it just to spite me!" my mother cried. At this moment she hated him as passionately as she had loved him.

"Two hundred is all I want," my father insisted.

"You could get thousands!" my mother shouted.

But two hundred was all he settled for, and the tramway company was happy to oblige.

My mother forced herself to accept the inevitable and talked about how she would spend the money. "I owe the milkman twenty dollars. I'll pay him back ten. The grocery store fifteen. We owe three months back rent. I'll pay back one. . . ."

On the day the cheque arrived, my father went to cash

it. Dinner time came and went but no Papa. The evening wore on and we were getting more anxious.

At last we heard a car pull up in front of the house. It was a taxi, and my father was dragging out wooden boxes, bags and placards.

"Our worries are over!" he exclaimed as he entered the house, hurling the bags and boxes.

"Where's the two hundred dollars?" my mother asked.

"We're going to be on easy street!" Papa shouted.

"Where's the two hundred dollars?"

Papa proudly displayed the placards which read: *Electric Milk Boxes — $1.00 EA*.

"This invention is going to sell like hotcakes!"

"Where's the two hundred dollars?"

Papa threw two ten-dollar bills on the table.

"That's twenty dollars." My mother's voice was becoming shriller.

"To make capital, you need capital!" my father explained. "It cost fifty dollars to get the right kind of wooden boxes that can hold four bottles of milk. The electric elements cost forty-seven dollars. The placards cost twenty-five dollars. It cost fifty dollars to patent it. The taxi cost eight dollars. That leaves twenty dollars. We're going to be millionaires!"

Placing the electric elements into boxes and grabbing a few of the placards, my father stormed out of the house to prove he had finally come up with a practical invention.

In Montreal the cold plunges to below zero and milk bottles left on doorsteps freeze and pop. Papa had lined his wooden boxes with asbestos so they wouldn't catch fire. The electric elements were attached to two sides and these to an electric cord which plugged into an outlet. You placed the milk bottles inside and they wouldn't freeze.

"Maybe *this* invention will sell," I said, trying to cheer up my mother.

But she just stared at the twenty dollars, and then at the wall.

During the next few days Papa distributed boxes to friends, relatives and neighbours, who promised to try out the invention. Each instructed the milkman to place the bottles inside the box.

Everyone supplied with a Webber Electric Milk Box no longer had milk that froze over. However, instead of freezing, the milk turned warm, so those who had Papa's boxes had warm milk for breakfast. If my father had known about thermostats. . . Well, but he didn't. And he never had the capital again to develop any of his inventions.

Looking for Bessie

I HADN'T SEEN MY MOTHER IN A FEW YEARS. IN the interim I'd gotten married, had a child and lived in New York. My parents still lived in Montreal where I'd been born. My mother hadn't met my wife or my child so when I sold a story to the movies for a lot of money, I telephoned her and said, "I've just sold a movie. I'm rich. I'd like you to come and visit us. I'll send you the plane tickets. When can you come?"

My mother said she couldn't come, as much as she wanted to see me and meet my wife and baby. Who would take care of my father? Besides, Uncle Willie and his two children were living with her again and there'd be nobody to cook for them. On top of that, she wouldn't take an airplane. She didn't believe in airplanes.

"I'll send you a return train ticket," I told her. I didn't want to hear any more nonsense about my father, who was old enough to take care of himself for a week. "And as far as Uncle Willie's kids are concerned, they're both in high school and can also take care of themselves."

There were a few more backs and forths and she finally agreed.

It was an exciting arrival. We all met her at the station. She said the pictures didn't do justice to either my wife or baby. They were really beautiful.

As soon as we got into the taxi, she said, "Give me the money to put in the bank for you. You'll pee it all away. Let me keep it for you so you'll have it."

I asked her to forget about money. My money worries were over for life. Besides, now that I had a wife and child, I didn't throw it around the way I had as a bachelor.

After she had spent time playing with the baby and we'd had our first supper together, I said, "Ma, please tell me what you want to do first. Do we start tomorrow on a shopping spree? Go along Fifth and Madison avenues and shop in all the famous stores? We'll walk along the aisles and you'll just point at something and we'll buy it. Gifts for yourself, for Pa, for Uncle Willie, my cousins, for Auntie Katie, anybody you want. Or would you rather we first went to a nightclub or a theatre? Or a movie? Radio City Music Hall? Something like that? You name it. What would you like to do first?"

"First I'd like to see Bessie."

"Who's Bessie?"

"You wouldn't remember Bessie. She knitted you a sweater when you were born. She's an old school friend of mine. She lives in the Bronx with her husband, Max. When I came to Uncle Joe's funeral here ten years ago, I visited her. I'd love to see Bessie. She was my best friend."

"Fine," I said. "Of course we'll see Bessie. But what do you want to do first? Shop or go to a nightclub or the theatre?"

"First I'd like to see Bessie," she repeated. "Would you phone her?"

"Of course I'll phone her. Do you have her number?"

"No. You'll have to get it from Information," said my mother.

"What's her name?"

"Her husband's name is Max. They live in the Bronx."

"What's her husband's second name?"

"I'm not sure. Zaratsky, Zatetsky, Zapitsky, something like that. Just ask Information."

"Which is it — Zatetsky, Zapitsky or Zaratsky?"

"I don't know," my mother said. "Just ask Information and don't make me nervous."

For the next thirty minutes I kept asking Information for the phone numbers of Max Zatetsky, Zapitsky or Zaratsky. I got quite a few who even had wives with the name of Bessie, but I never got the right one.

"Maybe they don't have a phone," I suggested.

"Bessie wouldn't be without a phone," said my mother.

"Maybe they moved."

"They wouldn't move. It's their own house."

I kept trying for more Zapitskys, Zaratskys and Zatetskys. I had started trying Zabutsky and Zalusky when my mother asked if I knew where Union Square was.

"Next door to Union Square is a department store called Klein's," she said.

"That's right."

"When Bessie took me shopping, we went to Klein's and we got off at the subway at Union Square."

"So?"

"If you took me to Union Square and I got into the subway, I'd find where she lives because we got off at a station with Point in it."

"Point in it?"

"Yes. I can't remember the name, but I remember it had Point in it."

"Huntspoint?"

"That's it," my mother said excitedly. "Huntspoint!"

"What if I had said Greenspoint?"

"No, it's Huntspoint. I remember now. Huntspoint," she said, not looking too certain.

Next morning was one of the hottest in the history of New York. By nine o'clock it had hit 96 degrees. My mother and I made our way towards Union Square.

"I just remembered the name of the street Bessie lives on," my mother announced. "Vine Street."

"That'll make it easier."

"Don't worry, we'll find her. I have a good head for these things. Once I found Jersey City all by myself."

We got to Union Square subway station. There was a queue. When I got to the man in the booth, I asked if he could tell me where Vine Street was. He looked in a little red book. "There is no Vine Street in Manhattan, Brooklyn, Bronx or Long Island."

"He doesn't know what he's talking about," my mother whispered to me.

"How do we get to Huntspoint?" I asked.

"Do you want Huntspoint Station or Huntspoint Avenue?" the man asked.

"Just Huntspoint," my mother said, staring back at him.

"Okay," said the man, "try Huntspoint Station," and he directed us to where we could get the Bronx local.

I read the *New York Times* standing in the subway, while my mother sat. She kept looking at the woman next to her. Finally she addressed her. "Do you live in the Bronx?"

The woman didn't reply. My mother continued, "Because if you live in the Bronx, I would ask you if you know my friend whose name is Bessie and whose husband's name is Max. They live in their own home on Vine Street with her two unmarried sister-in-laws."

The woman turned so that her back was almost to my mother. My mother pulled at my jacket and whispered, "She must be a deaf mute."

We got off at Huntspoint Station. There were not two streets crossing one another but three, so that there were six different streets intersecting.

"This is it," my mother proclaimed, her eyes shining happily. "I remember it well!" She headed straight down a thoroughfare.

She surveyed the area with a grand sweep of her eyes. There were the usual shops — delicatessen, grocery, fruit, bakery, kosher butcher. This was most definitely the neighbourhood where she and her friend Bessie had shopped during my mother's short visit a dozen years ago. Her excitement grew.

"This is the neighbourhood, all right. This is where we shopped."

We walked down one block, looking for Vine Street. Although the houses were painted in different colours, the array of duplexes and small patches of garden was of a monotonous sameness. "Think you'll remember the house?"

My mother didn't think it necessary to reply and ploughed forward. We retraced our steps to go down another street that looked more or less like the one we'd already been on. Then another. And then another. But still no Vine Street.

"Are you sure this was the right subway stop?" I asked foolishly.

"Come," she said, pushing onward.

The heat was murderous. We had passed into scorching afternoon.

"To be so close. . ." my mother sighed. "If Bessie knew I was this close. . ."

Down another block, down another block.

I was alone. I'd been talking to my mother but she had disappeared. I had lost my mother. I looked in every direction. No mother.

I retraced my steps, looking into shops we had passed, a delicatessen, a bakery, a fruit store. . . . No mother. Finally I spotted her inside a small grocery store near the corner.

The woman behind the counter was saying, "I know a lot of Bessies but not that one."

"She lives in her own home with her two unmarried sister-in-laws who live upstairs," my mother said. "Her husband's name is Max."

The woman shook her head. "No, I don't know."

"They're not a friendly people here," my mother remarked to me.

I apologized to the woman behind the counter and led my mother to the door.

"Everybody warned me New Yorkers are not friendly," she said gloomily. "In Montreal everybody knows me. Especially where I shop. Bessie and I used to come to that grocery store every day, and now they don't even remember her. They're not a friendly people here."

By now the heat was unbearable. "Mama, I've had it," I said finally. "Let's go home."

But she refused to accept defeat and marched into a launderette. The middle-aged owner was behind the counter reading a newspaper. Mother tried to make herself heard above the noisy washing machines.

"Could you please tell us," she shouted, "where Vine Street is? I know it's around here somewhere."

He looked up as if he had still not heard.

"Vine Street. Could you please tell me where it is?"

"Lady," he growled, "I've lived in this neighbourhood for twenty-five years and I never heard of Vine Street."

As we left the shop, my mother was mimicking him under her breath.

Next time I make some money, I vowed to myself, I'll send it to my mother and let her stay home.

"To be so close," she sighed again, "and not find Bessie."

We were making our way to the subway station when she stopped in the middle of the street. "Wait, I have a feeling. . ." She closed her eyes, then opened them.

"Those doors," she said, pointing to a nearby red garage. "Max used to keep his car in that garage!"

My mother headed for the red garage, and I followed. We came to a corner where a sign read, "Irvine Street."

96

"This is it!" my mother shouted, walking with authority.

"I thought you said Vine Street."

"So I made a mistake."

"Will you remember the house?"

"Of course!" she said impatiently.

It was almost dusk. People were trying to escape the heat on stairways and porches.

Out of the dimness suddenly came a woman's surprised voice. "Annie!"

My mother turned.

"Bessie!"

They ran into each other's arms.

Then my mother turned and said, "See?"

That's the story. But there's a postscript. That night, after we got home from Bessie's, where we had met Max and Bessie's two unmarried sisters-in-law, and we had told the story a hundred times to my wife and friends who were visiting, the family went to sleep and I remained in the kitchen to type out the story.

Next morning when I came for breakfast, my mother was sitting at the table reading the pages. She looked puzzled as I walked in. "This is what we did yesterday."

I nodded and poured some coffee.

"Why did you write it down?"

"It's a funny story," I said.

"All right, but why did you write it down? It's just what we did yesterday!"

"I'll send it to a magazine and perhaps they'll buy it." I said.

"Buy it?" She stared at me. "They pay money for such things?"

I nodded.

"If that's the case," she said, "sit down and I'll tell you what I did the day before yesterday."

The Moon to Play With

I SEEMED TO BE THE ONLY ONE WHO HAD ANY control over my father during his manic phases. Otherwise, my mother managed to keep him from roaming through the neighbourhood and frightening the neighbours. Today he was standing on the sidewalk shouting obscenities at passers-by. He was so outrageous that my mother telephoned and asked if I could come over.

At the time, I was writing radio and television plays and had become prominent enough to appear on an occasional talk show. I was rapidly getting the reputation of being a raconteur and wit. My father was the big cloud on my horizon.

When I arrived at my parents' small duplex on that residential middle-class street, I was relieved that my father was nowhere in sight. During my teens, he'd greet me when I was coming home from school by standing inside a full rain barrel, fully dressed, soaking wet, grinning and shouting, "Howdje do! Here comes my brilliant son!" And he'd call out my name. I'd repress my anger, grab his arm and help him get out of the flooded barrel. On such occasions he was good-natured and giggly.

But the memory that comes to me now was of a different sort.

"Where is he?" I asked my mother.

"In the backyard burning garbage. All he does is burn garbage."

"How bad is he?"

"Bad. But in the evening he gets quieter. You think I should put him away before he gets into trouble?"

"Are you worried being here alone with him? Shall I sleep over a few nights?"

"It's funny, but I'm not afraid to be with him now because of Blackie."

She was holding the little cocker spaniel I'd given her a few months before. She had never liked dogs, and when Joel and I were children she'd never allowed us to have one. But Blackie was different. Why, she couldn't explain. He was a beautiful dog, gentle and well-behaved. He never dirtied the house. And he worshipped her. "He's like a child to me," she'd say happily.

The dog drowsed in her lap. "Pa wanted to buy you kids a dog but I wouldn't let him. I don't know why. I never thought I could love a dog." She patted its head, and the tail started wagging.

My father walked in. "That damn dog is barking too much," he shouted. "Every time a person passes, this idiot barks."

"He's not making a sound. David's here. Why don't you say hello to him?"

"Hello, genius. Making millions?" He let out a crazy cackle.

"Stop laughing like that," my mother said. "You give me the shivers."

"Go lie down and rest," I said.

"He's got a potbelly now so he thinks he can boss me around." My father walked out of the house.

"Where are you going at this hour?" my mother shouted.

"Go piss on a piano!" he shouted back.

She gasped and held her breath. "It's such a shame for the neighbours. This is the worst he's been this week."

In the backyard he was singing a lullaby he'd sung to my kid brother Joel and me when we were kids.

> *"Lula lula lula lula bye-bye*
> *Do you want the moon to play with?*
> *Or the stars to run away with?*
> *They'll come if you don't cry."*

"He gives me the willies when he sings that song. But let him sing," I said. "He's happy."

"Joel says I should put him away."

"Joel still so busy?"

"Sure he's busy," she said proudly. "His factory's working overtime. He's making very good. He just bought a new car. When I hear how you and Joel are making good, I gain ten pounds. If only Pa would be well, I'd be the happiest woman alive. Now that we're old and we could be so happy, it has to happen to him again. Why am I so unlucky?"

"What does he do all day?"

"He writes."

"What?"

"He sits at the table with sheets of paper and stares at a page. Then he turns it over and stares at the next page. He says he's writing with his eyes."

I imagined him looking at the blank sheets of paper. I opened the back door. He was gazing up at the night sky.

"Why don't you use a pen when you write?"

He continued to stare up at the stars without replying. I was about to close the door when he turned and said, "Because I do not choose to share."

"He might be writing masterpieces for all we know."

My mother nodded. "How is it a mind like his, he's so

intelligent a man, should get so foolish? He could have been one of the richest men in the city if he hadn't taken sick every few years. Remember that toy factory he had when you were a little boy? And later the big clothing factory. But always with these breakdowns. Imagine, his own brother told me they had to put him in a mental hospital when he was seventeen."

"You've told me that a million times!"

"What are you getting mad about?" she asked. "So I told it to you again. Is that a reason to shout at me?"

I watched the sleeping dog in my mother's lap, wondering why I had gotten so angry. The truth was my mother often got on my nerves. I felt calm and loving enough when I first saw her, but after a while I found it unnerving to be with her.

I went into the backyard to say good-bye to my father. He was looking at the moon and raving. "We're all finished, the bunch of us, the father, the sons and the holy ghosts one bigger than the other, no guts, no guts, the frightened women making us bigger assholes and us so full of it and still wondering why they're sleeping around with the whores a bunch of manure piles all of us the men as well as the women whores sluts and cunts. . ."

The bastard, I thought. He's doing that for my benefit.

He knew that during the early years of my marriage I had been pathologically jealous and had accused my wife of infidelities. After many years of therapy, I had connected my state of mind with my father raving about my mother and that all women were whores.

"No kidneys veal cutlets or breast of chicken no mincemeat no pussy no nooky no eggs no balls and no brains." Then he started singing, "I wonder who's kissing her now. . ."

"Good night," I said.

My father eyed me with a meaningful, secretive grin. "If

music be the food of love, play on, eh, Davie boy?"

"I'll be around this weekend. Stop putting on this stupid act and frightening Ma. Take care of her. Her heart's not good."

"She takes good care of herself. You take care of Myra better. How is she?"

He always does this, I thought. From a raving maniac to a sensible human being.

"She's in bed with the flu."

"Myra never had much use for being on her feet anyway," he cackled. "She always preferred lying on her back."

I drove off, hearing my father's crazy laughter in my ears.

I didn't sleep much that night. Memory and dream merged. I'd fall asleep fitfully, awake sweating and lie there remembering.

Thirty years back. I was ten. He was sick again. My mother gave him sleeping pills at night but he awoke at dawn and started harassing her. "You wrecked us all! You wrecked us, so why shouldn't I wreck you?"

"Stop talking so loud. You'll wake the children."

"Money! Money! Money! Money! Money! Money!" he taunted.

"Harry, you'll wake the children! Take another pill."

"I know what you're thinking!" he shouted. "I know what you're all thinking. Don't try and lock me up again! If you do it once more, I'll cut your throat."

He began banging pots on the wall. She cursed him and cried to pull the aluminum ware from his hands. "I hate you when you get like this!" she cried. "You don't give a damn for the children! I hate you!"

"Step this way and see the red-hot mommas!" he started shouting. "See the momsters eating their children. Halle-

103

lujah brothers and sisters! Go down Moses and let my people go! Momster! Devourer! RRRRR. Rrr-rrr," he growled like a dog.

Then he became silent and we listened, our bodies tense. We could hear his quieter, normal voice. "It's not your fault. All men are trapped. Cunts trap them. You can't be blamed personally for it."

There was silence. Then came the voice we loved, the storytelling voice. "Did I wake you?" he asked gently. "I'm sorry." Another silence, which we interpreted to mean our mother was hugging him.

"I love you so much, Harry," she said. Then she burst into sobs. "I loved you so much," she kept sobbing. "You were such a wonderful man! Please get well. Get well so we can make love again and walk in the park. . . ."

Her heartbreaking sobs filled the house. We held our hands to our ears. I was ten. Sarah was eight. Joel was six.

"Dead they speak of him as. And not a smell of rot to show the way yet," my father intoned.

> *"Blow, blow, the breezes blow*
> *And little fleas all want to know*
> *Who are the giants that come and go*
> *And smell so, and smell so."*

And the stories he told us every night and the songs he sang. My favourite, "The Moon to Play With," flooded through me.

Next day my mother phoned. He was getting more violent. He had broken some kitchen chairs and hammered a hodge-podge of pieces nailed together which he called his "prison." Blackie had gotten in his way and he had kicked the animal, making it howl in pain. When she had protested, he snarled, "Get out of my way both of you! Just keep out of my way!"

104

When I got there she was pale. "He's very bad this evening," she said.

He was in the workshed building his "prison," hammering away. He came in for supper, paying no attention to me. She had prepared a cabbage soup which he sipped, mumbling about evolution and man and woman and war and money. "I remember when I was a savage in Africa after I'd been a child in the jungle and we drank human blood. That was an honest way to drink the blood of one's fellow man, not like today when they're going to burn us all with H-bombs."

He suddenly grabbed the pot on the stove and dumped its contents to the floor, swinging the pot at the wall and screaming, "Burn! Burn! Burn! This time the furnaces will be for all! No gas chambers will be needed! Scorched earth and flesh and every living thing dead, blackened burnt death!"

Two more such days passed. I'd called Myra to tell her what was happening. Why were we delaying calling the hospital and having attendants come and get him? I explained my mother kept hoping he'd take a turn for the better.

I'd moved my typewriter into my old bedroom and worked there, coming out whenever he sounded too violent, hoping my presence would calm him. But it didn't seem to make any difference. If anything, I think he acted more wildly when he had a bigger audience.

On the fourth day my mother was darning his socks and I had left my room to prepare tea when he walked in through the front door and stood silently before her. His mouth seemed dry and he kept wetting his lips.

"Don't feel too bad about it," he said.

"You'll get well. The worst is over."

"About Blackie," he said.

She placed the wool on the table beside her and stood up.

"A car just ran over him. He's dead."

I followed my mother running out of the house. Blackie was lying in a blanket of blood on the street just in front of the house. A group of children had gathered around and a man came to us. "I feel terrible. I love dogs. I feel just terrible. But he ran right under my car."

My mother walked to the dog and stood beside him. One of the children said, "The blood is thick like paste." Then my mother returned to the house and sat down. "It's crazy," she said half to herself. "It's crazy to feel this way about a dog."

She seemed to find it hard to breathe. We looked out the window. My father was dragging Blackie to the side of the street and covered it with a sack.

"He feels bad," she said softly. "He feels bad for me. But it's crazy to feel like this over a dog."

Blackie was taken away a few hours later and my mother sat rocking back and forth in grief.

My father remained quiet the rest of the day and when he came in, he just stared and said nothing.

"The dog's made him sad," she whispered when he disappeared into the bathroom. "Maybe it had to happen this way. Maybe Blackie's dying will make him well. Maybe for something good to happen, something bad has to happen."

Next day my mother expressed the same hopes. "I can't stand it when he's in that place. He was noisy again this morning, but I think he's getting better. Do you think so?"

I nodded. "He does seem a little quieter."

It was then that we heard his insane laugh again. We heard him talking in the backyard. We both looked out and saw that he was speaking with Mrs. Kenwood, the neighbour to the right. She was nodding her head and trying to break off the conversation, but my father kept talking.

"She loved that dog," he said. "She sure loved that dog."

"Yes, I know," Mrs. Kenwood remarked. "He was a

sweet dog. I saw it happen. It was terrible."

"A dog is a dog," my father said. "He barked too much. The idiot barked at everything that passed."

"Is that why you called him?" Mrs. Kenwood asked.

"Sure. I called him because he was barking."

"But didn't you see that car coming?"

"Sure, I saw it coming!" he shouted gleefully.

My mother had her hand over her open mouth. "I'll put him away now," she said hoarsely. "I'll put him away and keep him there until he rots!" She uttered the words with a hatred I'd never heard her express, sobbing and holding her stomach in pain. "Until he rots, until he rots!"

He started singing again after Mrs. Kenwood returned to her house.

"I feel like taking a knife and killing him," my mother whispered. "I've never hated anybody like I hate him now."

He walked in and stared at her. She could not stop crying.

"It's just a dog," he said.

"We heard what you told Mrs. Kenwood. We heard!" she screamed. "We heard how you called him when you saw the car coming!"

He looked troubled. "It's just a dog," he repeated, a hurt, trapped look on his face.

"I loved him," she sobbed. "I loved him. You knew that. Why did you want to hurt me like that?"

"You loved that dog too much." He looked troubled and confused. "You would have sent me away. You'll be lonely now if you send me away."

"Go away!" she shouted. "Get out of my sight!"

My father went back to the garden and kept looking towards the house with a worried expression, and then he started singing softly to himself.

> *"Do you want the moon to play with?*
> *Or the stars to run away with?*
> *They'll come if you don't cry."*

Testament of a Maniac

Sunday

Dear Dr. Belmore:

Thank you, thank you for letting me have a typewriter and a room for myself. The window is open and spring is singing so loudly it makes my head whirl. I've always had difficulty expressing myself speaking and this is rather clever of you *and* the Committee. I'll probably get well faster this way and at the same time the Committee will get the information it wants. This is very good for it kills two crazy birds in my head with one stone.

As I write this I'm feeling calm and rational and don't have the cramps I've been having getting up these past mornings. I don't have those frightening images in my head either, so it looks like I'm getting off to a promising start.

I had to stop just then because I laughed. I'll make a sign like this :::: when I stop to laugh so you'll always know exactly how I'm feeling. I'll make a sign like this ----// if I should have to stop to cry.

I think we understand each other. I know why you gave me this typewriter and I will not disappoint you. Even if I didn't write another sentence I think I've proved that I do trust you and we'll probably be very good friends after I become sane again.

It will be easier now to explain about my testimony before the Committee for I never wanted to be unfriendly to anyone, least of all a committee representing the Congress of the United States.

I know that I'm to blame for everything that's happened to me. I know now I was a dupe and a fool.

I knew I was a traitor after the Committee chairman explained it to me and I *wanted* to name names and expose all those people I knew had been communists when I attended meetings during the thirties and was so confused about fascism and unemployment (all *those* clichés!). I mean I knew I should have co-operated and exposed them all but I was already sick by then and I couldn't remember their names and this is what I'd like the Committee to understand. If I hadn't been sick I'd have remembered. If I could finally make this clear I'd feel better about everything.

My wife understands me, which has had its disadvantages. (I *mean* this to be funny.) When she visited me last month (I understand about her not being able to visit more often, that she's busy, it takes a long time to get here, etc. etc. etc. etc.). I explained everything to her, for the first time really. She keeps asking me why I have that smile on my face when I talk to her. You know why I have to smile when I'm with her. She really thinks she believes what she's saying and it makes me smile. I told her to get a divorce and marry Sydney. She's had a "thing" for Sydney for a long time now and he's making a very good living and will be able to support her much better than I ever did. Myra's quite frightened about being economically insecure and I had all those illusions I told you about concerning my talents as a writer which made things pretty tough for her.

I'm not going to let this get sad or morbid in any way, but that pressure in the front part of my head, just above my right eye, is coming back now. It always does when I think of my mother or Myra. I *do* get the connection. Honestly, I do. I think psychiatry and psychoanalysis pretty wonderful to show how one's childhood attitudes to one's parents and their attitudes towards you (particularly their terrible hostility) determine behaviour the rest of one's life. I think this is a very important contribution to human progress and I am sure it will help get me well as soon as I can start using my intelligence in a healthy manner. I know Myra is very much like my mother. If she wasn't to begin with, I made her become very much like my mother. I can see that now, but I do wish to hell all this had been known when my grandparents were alive. I know I'd have felt a lot different about a lot of things if my grandparents hadn't done to my parents what they did. I feel they took it out on me. My parents took it out on me, I mean.

It will surprise a lot of people, I think, if you ever show them what I'm writing, to realize that a man who is mentally ill *knows* he is mentally ill and can write about it with some degree of lucidity. I think this can help the whole field of psychiatry and lead to greater understanding of human behaviour. I am very anxious that there should be a greater understanding of human behaviour, particularly mine.

Monday morning

I developed a severe headache while typing yesterday and I decided to stop. There were quite a few visitors and the noise bothered me. My mother always screamed. I think I've told you that. Anyway, there are times I know that my belief that I love people is a terrible lie. I hated people yesterday. I mean *literally* hated them enough to want to kill them. It is because I know I have such thoughts that I realized the members of the Committee were right to

111

suspect me about everything. They thought the only thing to investigate about my going to Spain was my belief in communism. It is even worse than that, and I cannot yet get myself to confess what *that* is. I will soon. Have patience with me. It'll come out, and please relay to them my promise that I will reveal everything about myself.

When I was in Spain I read an article about the International Brigade by some party-line hack and he called them "the cream of the world." I felt very good about this because it built up my self-esteem. Now I know we were dirty commies and traitors and adventurers trying to impose a cruel dictatorship on Spain. But I didn't know that *then*. I thought we were fighting to *prevent* a cruel dictatorship. The Committee should try to understand that.

Monday afternoon

It *was* very clever of you to get me this typewriter for I'd never have been able to have explained all this verbally.

For the Committee to fully understand, they *should* know everything about my past, but I'm not going to go into sex during adolescence and all that sort of thing. I did masturbate, as I've told you quite a few times. (If you do want to publish this in any of the medical journals, I really don't mind if you use my right name because most people don't know me by that. Just don't use my pseudonym.) I was damned miserable and wanted to die half of the time. I kept hoping I had a beautiful soul. I kept hoping I was the sort of person who could be Christ-like and love everyone and suffer for everyone and not need anyone to love him in return. I did so much want to be pure and good and beautiful a person inside, but I couldn't. I used to wake up mornings praying that just for that day alone if I could be a good person in every possible way it would be enough for me. But I never made it. Not even for a day. I think I

112

was really beautiful inside and full of love for about an hour. I needed to be loved so desperately it makes me cry now just to think of it. God, I really was maudlin and disgusting. I was a great trial to Mother and I made her very nervous. She used to hit me across the face quite often, particularly when I expressed an opinion she didn't like. I'm not blaming her for this (my father did, but he hated her, so one cannot pay any attention to his observations about her) but that's what made it difficult to confess the one thing about me that's even worse than being a communist. I mean the time I grabbed my mother's wrist (I was fourteen) and said that if she hit me once more I'd kill her. I have felt very guilty about this ever since. She really didn't like me, but she kept making me think I was her favourite and this gave me terrible headaches. I mean she kept hitting me and screaming and then telling me she liked me and I suppose the poor woman was very confused. I certainly don't want the Committee to think I'm criticizing my mother in any way. I read the other day where the Committee chairman said you could have many wives but you could only have one mother. To show you how sick I am, I thought: That's really too bad.

It is clear that if a child can't love its own mother, it's not going to grow up into a very solid citizen, is it?

I think one of the reasons I started going to communist meetings was to spite my mother. If one is going to spite one's very own mother, then one deserves everything he's going to get. And you know I've never once said I didn't deserve everything I got.

My mother used to tell me that I had been a very beautiful child. She could never understand how someone who'd been such a beautiful baby could change the way I did. I started hating God for making me so ugly, and that led me to atheism. In my teens some cruel girls said I was handsome. I wanted to kill myself because I never believed

113

people could be as cruel as that, to tease me like that. I couldn't help being ugly, could I? To this day there are women who are so sick and whose need to hurt so deep they go out of their way to tell me I'm handsome. This kind of teasing used to make me cry, but now I joke right back at them. I really don't get hurt by it now, but I think those types should get psychoanalyzed to find out what makes them so cruel.

:::: I'm feeling good and not affected by these things anymore. I'm not an adolescent, after all. I'm a man of forty now and things like that roll off my back. I really do not care that I'm not an attractive person outside. All those women can go to hell! I s--t on them all! ::::

(I had to laugh.)

Tuesday

I was always over-emotional about everything. Once I saw a kid with a swollen belly and somebody said it was starving. In our country! I bawled. I started crying and ran back to my house and got some bread and a banana and I gave it to the kid and I wanted to die thinking of all the food I'd eaten and this kid was dying of hunger. God, I get sick thinking of it to this day. Then during the depression and all those unemployed and I was unemployed too and the police hitting us over the head when we had demonstrations. I'd like to explain about those demonstrations. We were hungry. I was just a kid in my teens then but a lot of those men had young children and they were easy marks for the communists who told them to come out into the streets and demand higher relief payments and all that malarkey. The commies just wanted to stir up trouble and I don't blame the police for trying to split our stupid heads open.

The Committee's information about my participation in that textile strike is not quite right. I never *led* the strike.

What happened was that I got this job and we were getting eight dollars a week. That was better than being unemployed and it was a sign of our neurotic behaviour that we weren't grateful, but other factories were paying sixteen dollars a week, and eight wasn't enough for a man with a family, and I had no family and the others were frightened so I agreed to be the spokesman for the section I worked in. I didn't *lead* the strike. God, we didn't want to strike. But we felt if we formed this union and asked the employer for a raise we'd get it. But the management said no and we went on strike and they tried to bring in scabs. That's where all this talk started about being an organizer. I wasn't. The men in my section figured I had no wife and kids and asked me to represent them. I said we shouldn't hit the scabs. I was always against violence. But the men on strike were fighting for a principle. I forget what the principle was now, but it seemed very important then.

Going to Spain was a different thing. When the fascists attacked in Spain and all the democratic countries said tant pis, too bad, so sorry, a lot of over-emotional neurotic types like myself thought we (the world) were being attacked by homicidal maniacs. I thought I was going there to defend myself and my loved ones. That was when I thought I had some loved ones.

I trusted Joseph Stalin. I believed he was gentle, modest and a "seeker after truth."

:::: I never believed those terrible stories about him. I thought they were all propaganda. So many terrible stories about Russia *were*, you know, that I couldn't tell what was true and what wasn't. I had a good friend whom I trusted. I can't remember his name now because of that block I have remembering the names of my friends who were communists. I'll call him Warren, but that's not his name so please tell the Committee not to question people just because their names are Warren. He'd visited Russia and told me they were building the future there *without lies*. You know how sick I feel when I find out anybody lies to me. Then Khrushchev made that speech about Stalin and I asked Warren about it because I couldn't believe it. But Warren said it seemed to be true. Then all those stories of Stalin's modesty and honesty were lies! My God. He actually went insane and that too was hidden from us. So what could anybody believe anymore? When my own father went insane I almost cracked up, but then I found the Party, and when that turned out to be sick and full of lies, I couldn't take it.

I had nothing and no one to turn to except myself. I know you said there is God to turn to, but I'm too sick to believe in a God, so it's all a vicious circle, isn't it? I understand the Russians sent a satellite into the universe which defies the laws of gravity and they've stopped killing anybody who disagrees with the Central Committee. All this might be a sign they're getting away from the lies, but I think I'll wait a little longer before sending love letters or marriage proposals.

I think I'm putting all this down rather well, don't you? I mean I'm convincing you and the Committee of my honesty, and I do hope nobody is going to start disliking me because of what I confessed about Spain. I think perhaps that after the war that's going to happen happens, I might get all better again. I might even start writing and getting published again.

Nurse Morris walked in just then and no doubt she'll be reporting she found me sitting at the typewriter and crying. Well, only you will know why. I wouldn't tell her. It was just then I remembered again that my father tried to jump out of a window.

Monday

I don't think I want to keep writing about Spain because that's why I haven't slept much these past nights. I'll try and get this thing over with. That town called Albacete. It's somewhere south of Madrid. It was a dirty, hot little town and fourteen German Heinkel bombers came over because it was where the International Brigade had its headquarters. I guess a couple of hundred people or thereabouts were killed. I was with a group that dug out bodies from the ruins and I touched the body of a dead child, a boy. I think he was about four years old. I tried to scratch the stones away from him and. I got over-emotional again, I suppose, and I kept hugging him, saying shh, shh, shh, shh, like he was asleep, but I knew he was dead and I felt I was not in my right mind. I think *that* was when I began to realize I was losing my mind. I thought: *Something happened to me once and I wonder what it is.*

I took the child and placed it on the sidewalk and forgot all about it. What *had* happened to me? You understand, don't you, that I didn't care about the dead child anymore, just about me. What *had* happened to me once, and why was my mind asking itself this question?

There were about ten of us digging in that group. We found twelve bodies and odd hands and feet. It was the first time any of us had ever been in a bombardment and the first time any of us had ever dug for bodies. Most of us vomited. I'm not trying to excuse my feelings. It's just that I didn't know what was the right thing to feel. There were no committees in those days to tell you the right thing to feel and I don't think I should be entirely blamed for feeling *some* of the things I did. But perhaps I am to blame. I get angry at myself when I start writing and thinking like I am now. I feel I'm making a fool of myself in your eyes.

Friday

I didn't feel like writing Thursday. It was cold. The radiators weren't working. The food was very bad. The potatoes were cold and soggy and the soup tasted like dishwater mixed with pepper. I don't like complaining about these things but I think you should know that the other patients in Ward H were very disturbed about the cold and the food.

Sunday

Thank you. I made Stanley promise he wouldn't threaten any of the attendants again. Thank you for letting him out of that place. I know it is very difficult to run a big hospital like this when so many of the patients do get violent. It must be a great relief for you to have a patient like me who still retains so much of his self-control.

Monday

That's a terrible bruise on Stanley's head. Nurse Morris says that Stanley is a trouble-maker and that I should watch myself or I'll become a trouble-maker too. *You* know me, doctor, and you know I don't want to be a trouble-maker. It makes me very depressed when somebody tells me a thing like that. Is it necessary for Nurse Morris to come around so often? She told me a couple of days ago that I undress her every time I look at her. The truth is I think she'd like to seduce me. When I feel a woman wants to seduce me, I start trying to seduce her right away, although I haven't made a move with Nurse Morris yet. I think if I seduced her, I could probably shut her up.

Tuesday

Do you show my writings to Nurse Morris?

Friday

I will try to do as you suggest, and thank you for the pills.
I think they do quieten me down. I wish I slept better,
though. The mornings are the worst time for me. When I
wake up I feel I'm living in a Nazi concentration camp and
I'm going to be led to the furnaces. I'll try not to evade
anymore. After Albacete I went back to Madrid and during
the bombings and shellings there, "it" would keep happening and I started getting disturbed. In the past when "it"
had happened, it didn't bother me. But now I became
frightened. (I get that same feeling when I hear Nurse
Morris' heels coming down the hall towards my room.) I
kept asking myself what happened in my mind to make
letters stick in the air this way. I felt myself getting more
and more psychotic.

I told you about that affair with the Spanish nurse,
Angela. We were going to get married but she was killed
during a bombardment so I had to change my plans. I
mean this to sound funny. It's important for you and
the committee to know that I never felt too badly about
Angela's death. I just thought, Poor Angela. She was only
twenty and so beautiful and now she's dead. . . . Sometimes
I feel I might have been different if Angela had not been
killed, but I don't know. I might have been different if
Franco had lost, but I don't know that either. I used to be
so sure about things like that, but now I'm not sure about
anything.

I left Spain a couple of months after Angela was killed. I
was writing newspaper articles by then and had given up
fighting. I hated coming home. My sense of humour went
out of control. I kept laughing at everything and couldn't
stop myself.

My mother considered me a failure. I hadn't learned any
trade and I still had illusions about becoming a writer.

119

Then World War II started and I volunteered. I was rejected because of a bad ear, though it didn't stop me from hearing the bombs drop in Spain. Anyway, I got a writing job for the government and felt I was doing my bit.

I tried to force myself to remember. What had happened to me? What terrible thing had happened which I couldn't remember? What if *nothing* had happened and it was just a cruel trick my mind was playing on me?

I became impossible to live with. My wife, Myra, urged me to see a psychiatrist and that was how I came to Dr. T. I said something to him about dead children under the ruins and the liars were the ones who destroyed childhood. I'm sure he must have sent you a report. I felt he didn't like me for having been a communist.

When I would read of an automobile accident, I'd feel sick and think, It might have been me. When I'd read of someone being hanged or electrocuted, I'd think, It might have been me. And then it got crazier and more frightening. When I read how the Nazis had gassed hundreds of thousands or burned them in the furnaces, I thought, That *was* me.

By the time the atom bomb dropped over Hiroshima and Nagasaki, I knew I was insane. Sometimes it frightened me, but other times it pleased me. I still feel this way. Being insane means I'm not responsible for what I say or do or think, and I like feeling that. I wouldn't do anything to harm anyone, but I feel good knowing I could kill somebody and I wouldn't be hanged for it. That shows the extent of my love for people and how despicable a person I really am. Perhaps you could drop a hint to Nurse Morris to leave me alone, that I might get violent and do her harm. She might try and be nicer to me if she was afraid. On the other hand, she might turn meaner. Better not tell her anything.

I had to stop then because Nurse Morris came in. She picks on me and will use any excuse to show me how much she dislikes me. Everyone in the hospital knows she reports everything she hears to the Committee. We know she's a spy. We all humour her along. Yesterday I told her I was Napoleon's Brandy. She didn't even get the joke. I just told her if she brought me hot soup tomorrow, I'd give her the names of five communists in the hospital administration. I won't name you, so don't start worrying about anything like that.

Monday

If it's true, as Nurse Morris says, that this is my last day to have the typewriter unless I remember those names, then you can go to hell. I don't need the damned typewriter anymore anyway. If I could remember the names and *consciously* co-operate, I'd be sane, wouldn't I? You're not such a good psychiatrist after all. I will now tell you something. We had a secret meeting of the patients in Ward H this morning. Tell that to the goddamned Committee and see how they like it. We passed a resolution unanimously (guess who proposed it?) calling upon all governments of the world who have the H-bomb to drop them on each other immediately. I suggested that such a resolution should come from a mental hospital, where most people running governments these days should be anyway. And I won't need the typewriter anymore because I'm not going to write another word or utter another word from this moment on. I don't have to. I just remembered what it was that happened to me. That child I found dead underneath the ruins in Albacete was me. Now that I know it, none of you can nag at me anymore. I'm dead, so nobody can hurt me again. :::: Hah, hah, hah. I get the last laugh, don't I? ::::::::

What Am I Doing Christmas?

I STOPPED AT A SWEETS SHOP TO BUY A FEW cartons of cigarettes for Sarah, as well as a two-pound box of chocolates. I had the dressing gown which my wife had bought on the family's behalf so I felt Sarah would not feel too neglected. The day was cloudy but mild, the countryside not at its best on such a day but still a welcome change from London's sunless, winter streets. The grounds of the huge sanatorium were large and impressive, with tennis courts, tree-lined walks and well-kept gardens.

It took about forty minutes, once you got to the highway from the Hammersmith overpass. My best friend, Charles, had come along for the ride. He had known Sarah when all of us had lived in Canada, but had never seen her ill. He asked me if he should come into the ward with me, and I replied that it was up to him but thought it just as well he didn't. If she was well enough, cheerful enough, she could come driving with us.

Charles took off his overcoat and sat in a large armchair in the lobby.

The place seemed better lit than the last time I had visited my sister. There were gaily painted posters with Christmas donation appeals. Friends of the sanatorium were going to run parties and present gifts to patients without friends or families.

I started looking for the ward Sarah was in, grateful Charles had come along for the ride. When my sister was in a manic state, she was very hostile.

As I made my way along the brown linoleum corridor lined with portraits of the sanatorium's founder and various benefactors, I compared it with all the other mental hospitals Sarah had been in. This was the best of the lot — spacious, permissive, no iron bars on windows, no locked doors. It was operated by private funds as well as government subsidy and there was probably nowhere outside of England one could get such facilities for so small a monthly fee.

I passed a bright therapy art studio with high-ceilinged windows, observing that some of the paintings were skilfully done. Someone was playing Bach in the music room. She will find friends here, I thought, and experienced a sense of satisfaction that I had found this place for her.

A young, well-groomed, dark-haired nurse met me and led me through a large social room off the ward, and then through the ward itself. She explained that Sarah was having tea and would be brought to me.

A few women sitting in the social room smiled as if they knew me. I nodded and returned the smiles, thinking they looked dead and Sarah shouldn't have to live with people like that. Depressed or manic, she was always alive, and surely they could arrange their wards where the "living" could mingle together. But perhaps the "dead" were only in a dead phase, and became alive again with time and treatment. I decided I'd better stop trying to judge and appraise everything. It was a fine place, the best I'd ever found for Sarah.

Last week someone had telephoned me from the hospital to say that inasmuch as there had been no improvement in

124

Sarah's condition for the past month, Dr. Penelope O'Brien thought that a mild dose of electric treatment might help her.

Before I had brought Sarah to this sanatorium, she had been in a severe manic state, raging at me because I had permitted other hospitals to administer electric shock treatment, which she described as a form of sadism and brutal coercion. She had been given shock treatment in the States without sedation or anaesthesia and was in terror of it. I had promised I would never give permission for electric shock again. In the meantime, a psychiatrist friend of mine had explained that modern methods of sedation and anaesthesia made it a completely untraumatic experience. He'd assured me that these days the patient wasn't conscious when the treatment was administered. This had shaken my resolve about never allowing her to get electric shock again.

I told the nurse I preferred to see Sarah before speaking to Dr. O'Brien. I waited in a small, cramped room which had French windows opening onto a neatly trimmed garden, but the windows were closed, despite the mild weather. I hung my coat, feeling that the place was overheated, and busied myself reading outdated magazines. I was getting nervous and tried to will myself into a state of calmness.

Then Sarah walked in, lean and bright-eyed, reminding me of how beautiful she had been. We embraced and I noted that her breath was unpleasant and there was the mild odour of body perspiration I associated with European women.

I showed her the Christmas packages I had brought, but she paid no attention. "I've stopped smoking," she said. "Isn't that nice?"

Pleased, I gaily placed the two cartons of cigarettes to one side.

She ignored the other gifts until I told her that one package contained a box of chocolates. "I'll give it to the nurse, to share with the other nurses," she said, and disappeared. When she returned, she seemed slightly distracted, patting her dress down and occasionally rubbing her hands.

"I have an appointment with Dr. O'Brien," I said, "and the question of E.S.T. has come up. Dr. O'Brien suggests a mild dose might be of help."

Sarah's face became grim. "No! No electric shock," she said emphatically. "I don't want it."

"Then you won't have it," I said, adding, "But isn't it possible a mild dose might help you get out of your depression more quickly?"

"No! I'm getting out of the depression without it. I don't want it! Why haven't you come to see me in all this time?"

I was surprised by the question. I had been in New York on business and had written her before I'd left to explain I'd be away for a few weeks. She said she never received the letter, which made me feel terrible, and I started explaining why I'd nad to leave London so suddenly, but she wasn't listening and I had a flash that she'd received the letter, but I kept on talking as if I believed her.

She suddenly interrupted me with the question, "Are you all right? Are you doing all right?"

"I'm doing fine. Why do you ask?"

"Have I caused you any trouble?"

Her face took on an exaggerated mask of concern, which didn't hide the real concern she was feeling about something. I wondered if it was anything she had created in fantasy, some hostile act against me.

"Have I caused you any trouble?" she asked again.

"What trouble do you think you caused me?" I asked, trying to hide my suspicion and anxiety.

"I don't know," she said, but she was evasive. I was tempted to cross-examine her, to find out what mischief

126

she might have started, but I decided to push it from my mind.

"What's going to happen to me?" she asked.

I tried not to let a note of impatience, anger or anxiety get into my voice. I spoke slowly, in a low, friendly voice, trying to remember the way my analyst had spoken to me years ago.

"Your basic problem," I told her, "is that you have never learned to take care of yourself, and so you get into one crisis after another, which leads either to manic highs or depressions. . . ."

"I find Dr. O'Brien very strange" was her comment after I'd concluded, although I hadn't mentioned the doctor once.

"In what way is she strange?"

"She took blood from my arm and had to inject the needle into me twice."

"That sometimes happens," I said, thinking that the doctor was apparently not one of the blessed ones. "It isn't easy to find a vein at the first stab."

"Dr. O'Brien hit me with a hammer all over my chest and arms," Sarah said accusingly.

"For your reflexes surely."

"Yes," she said, "it was a rubber hammer, but I find Dr. O'Brien a strange person."

"Do you consider her intelligent?"

"I don't know."

The nurse came in to tell me Dr. O'Brien could see me now. Her office was directly across the corridor from the small waiting room. She was a woman in her thirties, with an attractive face and short legs with thick ankles. She exuded a feeling of confidence.

"Who," she said pleasantly, "has asked to see whom?"

I said I'd been telephoned and was under the impression she had wanted to see me, but that I didn't mind seeing her and was quite prepared to let her know what I thought of the situation. I concentrated on being relaxed, recalling that once when I was about twenty and had gone to visit Sarah at some state hospital in the United States, I'd sneaked a look at the doctor's desk and read the report in which I was described as "an hysterical type." That was over twenty years ago, I reminded myself. Now I'm a mature man, relaxed, in control, established in my profession. Many years and events have passed since I could be described as hysterical, and if you considered that the whole responsibility for Sarah had been put on my shoulders when I was only eighteen. . .

I brought myself back into focus.

"During the first few weeks Sarah was here, I tried to press her to take shock treatment," Dr. O'Brien was saying. "Had she agreed, it might have removed her irrational fears about it. However, she will not be given any electric treatments for the time being."

I expressed my pleasure with her decision and was conscious that I was trying to impress her with my charm and intelligence, my sense of humour, my understanding.

I explained that I considered the problem as much a social as a psychological one. Sarah needed an environment which stimulated her and in which she could feel secure. I told her how I'd been delegated to take care of my little sister since I was four, how I'd resented this, repressed this resentment and felt guilty about my ambivalence.

I explained how Sarah and I had loved each other since adolescence, that we had considered each to be the other's best friend, that she had gone into a manic high at the age of sixteen, and our father had taken one of his periodic trips out of town, that our mother was hysterical, that I was delegated by my mother and family doctor to get Sarah to a mental hospital or else the police would come and take her forcibly, that I hadn't known what to do and had asked a friend to give me some knockout drops and had given them to Sarah and told her I was taking her to a dance, and she had told me I was the only person in the world she could trust. I brought her to a mental hospital near Montreal, which was one of the scandals and hellholes of North America, but I hadn't known that then. And she had said what a strange place for a dance, and I had run, and she had awakened next morning in a straitjacket in this insane asylum. . . .

I couldn't stop talking and said I'd felt guilty about Sarah ever since because I believed I had ruined her life. "But I've learned a lot in analysis," I heard myself saying, "and I don't try to repress my feelings of guilt anymore. I don't want to see Sarah regularly. I've always visited her every weekend when she was in hospital, and I'm not going to do this anymore."

This time when she came out of hospital, I would ask the mental aftercare people to take care of her. I'd seen an advertisement by this organization and I'd gone to their offices and they seemed helpful and intelligent.

"Sarah will have to be told all this," I said. "My family feels burdened by her. She upsets my children, my wife, my personal life, and I have to take a rational step now, and she will have to be told this."

"By whom?" asked Dr. O'Brien.

"By me," I said, showing her how prepared I was to face the problem. "Should I tell Sarah now or would it be better to wait until she was feeling stronger?"

"I think you should tell Sarah *now*, so she'll start to learn to cope with it during hospital."

I nodded, not sure I agreed with Dr. O'Brien, and then she surprised me by asking, "Do you think you are good for your sister?"

I burst into laughter. "No," I said, "I'm very bad for her," and then, to give a clearer example of why I was especially bad for her, I revealed something I'd forgotten when I received the call from the hospital about the electric treatments. "My first thought," I told Dr. O'Brien, "was, Good grief! She'll get better and be on my hands again! And not only that," I continued, revelling in the confession, "there is something in me that wants her ill and dependent on me."

Dr. O'Brien nodded and smiled.

"Sarah's reaction to my suggestion that she go into an industrial therapy set-up was rather interesting," said Dr. O'Brien. " 'I'll talk to my brother about *that*!' said Sarah. This is so unusual that I wondered at it."

We both lit cigarettes and I stretched my legs. We were now like two doctors discussing a case. I'd succeeded in being calm and objective, after all, creating the image of myself I had wanted to. "Yes," I said, inhaling and letting the smoke out slowly, for I was thinking clearly and wanted it known that I was choosing my words carefully. "To Sarah, I, her older brother, am both protector and punisher. I would either say, 'Nobody can do this to my little sister!' or, 'You have to go!' She'd either go, feeling punished, or rebel."

"Yes," nodded the doctor, pushing the ashtray closer so I wouldn't have to reach so far. "Yes, of course."

The atmosphere seemed cosy now, almost intimate, like two old university colleagues meeting after a long separation and discussing various cases they happened to have treated, she in her capacity as hospital psychiatrist, I as consultant. I felt I could now reveal what Sarah had said about the blood-letting and hammer-hitting.

Dr. O'Brien looked puzzled. "That's very interesting," she said, "for Sarah seemed so remote, so dissociated when

I was doing it, I hardly thought she noticed anything."

"She notices everything," I said in the tone of the older doctor-consultant, "and remembers everything."

Dr. O'Brien confessed she had no idea what was going on with Sarah, "except theoretically I know that during a depression a patient is full of hostility which is repressed."

"I think Sarah is still full of tremendous hostility," I concurred, "mostly directed at me, which probably confuses her terribly. Here I am the only one who tries to take care of her, who ever visits her, and she has this hostility towards me. I think I should point out," I added, knowing that what I was about to reveal would make an even greater impression on Dr. O'Brien, "that I'm not feeling as reasonable as I sound. I am still involved with Sarah, still angry about it, about her hostility, although I realize this is silly and Sarah cannot help herself."

"That's understandable," Dr. O'Brien said, and I felt that the interview had gone very well. She then summed up what Sarah's needs would be after she left the hospital: "One, protective environment, and two, discipline."

"I can add a third," I said, feeling superior. "Stimulating environment."

"That," said Dr. O'Brien, "is difficult to find."

I agreed and rose to go. Dr. O'Brien said she had suggested to Sarah that she get into more activity and Sarah had not liked the suggestion. "But I will transfer her to another ward where the patients are more active."

I crossed to the small waiting room and greeted my sister. The session with the doctor had given me confidence. I felt I could cope with Sarah on every level and still be kind. I could even handle her hostility.

My first words were a trifle too cheerful. "Dr. O'Brien no longer feels that electric treatment is necessary because you've improved so much. Isn't that nice? So there was no argument about it at all. And now I'd really like to speak to you about some things which would be good for you to think about."

I then launched in, speaking softly, which was not always easy for me, and slowly, which was even more difficult, explaining the origins of my anger, hostility and resentment about our relationship. I spoke of her needs and problems, summing up what Dr. O'Brien and I had concluded. I urged Sarah not to repress her hostility but to let it come out where it could be examined and used constructively. She looked hurt when I reminded her how hostile she had been the day I brought her to the sanatorium and said she hadn't meant it, I shouldn't be angry.

"But I'm *not* angry about it," I insisted, pleased that I sounded gentle. "And you mustn't feel ashamed of your hostility. It will be good for you," I heard myself saying, and wondering what I was raving about. But she wasn't paying attention, for she suddenly asked, "Why have you brought me Christmas gifts so early?"

"It's December *fourteenth*."

"Am I never going to see you again?" she asked.

"Of course. But not necessarily *before* Christmas. I *might* see you before, but I'm so busy now I might not be able to see you until *after* the Christmas holidays. I'll write and let you know." I forced myself to look straight at her. She was to see that I was now strong and would not waver from my position, as I had so often in the past.

She studied me as if trying to puzzle out what I was saying, then asked the question again, "What's going to happen to me?"

I suppressed the emotions which were trying to surface and outlined her possible future. I put the required tone of enthusiasm and hope into my voice, predicting she would soon leave the hospital. She would then go into a mental aftercare hostel, which I was investigating. These were places created precisely for people like Sarah who had no families to go to. She would then live as useful and as happy a life as possible. She should no longer expect to see me regularly.

I looked at my watch, unable to hold her stare. I said I had to go.

"You've hardly been here," she cried, then went into a whispered incantation of agony. "Please, please don't leave me. Please. . ."

"If you make a scene whenever I start to leave, it makes it more difficult for me to visit you." I was unable to control the impatience in my voice, thinking I must concentrate and not let her pathetic chant depress me.

"Please, please don't leave me," she kept pleading in that childlike whimper.

"I have to go." I felt ill for her and put on my overcoat. "I have work to do. Can't you understand that? It takes an hour and a half to get here. It takes an hour and a half to get home. I have financial problems and time problems. . . ."

"I made out a list of things I need," she said in a small voice. "Sister Kingston said I should give you the list."

"I'm in a hurry," I said, "so please get the list."

I started for the door, and she followed. We walked down a long corridor towards her ward. We passed patients in various stages of listlessness, and then a large full-length mirror. I noticed that she took a quick look at herself as we passed. This seemed so incongruous after her childlike cries that I reached over to give her a pat on the cheek. Sarah knew I was being playful but wouldn't join. She looked at me as if she didn't understand my gesture.

She got the list from a small white-painted chest beside her bed. I counted seven more beds in the ward, some with women asleep or resting. One of them said hello and Sarah whispered, "She's in a very hostile state and keeps us awake at night."

"You should ask her to reserve her hostility for the daytime," I bantered.

"I'll ask her," said Sarah, a hint of a smile on her face.

I examined the list, which consisted mostly of her winter clothing which I had stored in my basement. At the bottom of the list was the word "money." I smiled and said I'd leave her some and send her a regular allowance to buy sweets or cigarettes if she started smoking again.

"I'll walk you to the entrance," she said.

"I'd rather you didn't," I said quickly, remembering the last time. "We'll say good-bye *here*."

A short, middle-aged woman in white approached, smiling cheerfully. Sarah introduced Sister Kingston and then said loudly and boastfully, "This is my brother, David."

Sister Kingston had a slight Edinburgh accent and stood firmly balanced on both feet, her stocky, peasant exterior reflecting a spirit at peace with itself. "Sarah forgot herself today," she announced, "and actually smiled."

I grinned, relieved at this cheerful interruption. "That's terrible," I said to Sarah. "Don't you dare smile again." She refused to join the exchange and put on her grim look again, so I turned to Sister Kingston. "Well, she's decided not to smile again," I said, adding that I'd send on Sarah's warm clothing and keep her supplied with a weekly allowance.

"Don't make it too much," the woman said. "She'll just spend it on the nurses and patients."

"I won't," said Sarah.

I walked through the ward and Sarah followed me until we came to another corridor. "I'm saying good-bye to you here," I said. She did not move, so I spoke more harshly. "Do you want *me* to make a scene here?"

"No," she said softly.

"Then go back."

Still she remained motionless, and finally said, "What am I doing Christmas?"

I didn't wait to take a breath. "You'll spend Christmas here. There'll be parties and all kinds of activities."

"I won't be spending it with you?"

"No. I've explained it all! I have to go."

She turned and walked back along the corridor now filling with patients who had returned from afternoon walks. I noticed that her bearing had suddenly become erect and her stride determined, as if she had made a decision not to cry.

When Everything Is Allowed

EVERYTHING IS A MATTER OF LUCK. *WHEN* A person is born, *who* his parents are, *what* happens to him. Some philosophers say it's free will. Others that it's destiny. I still call it "luck."

I was lucky in regard to my mother, unlucky as far as my father was concerned. My mother was different from other mothers. She not only spoke to God but also to the dead. It was not a matter of her *imagining* anything. She had long conversations with her dead mother and, after my grandfather died, she'd talk to him as well. She also had prophetic dreams, and once when I was sick with typhoid fever she dreamed I had blood in my stool and telephoned New York from Montreal. I was in the hospital, so she spoke to my wife.

"I had a dream that David is sick," my mother told her.

"Yes," my wife said, "he's very sick. He's dying."

"He won't die," my mother said. "He got better in the dream."

The doctors had told Myra I was going to die any day or night that week, so it was obvious my mother was right and the doctors wrong. I'm not dead yet. I'll be dying soon because of a bad heart attack I had a few years back, but I don't mind that. When I speak to my mother she tells me

I'll be joining her soon but doesn't know exactly when. She died about ten years ago and we have many conversations, usually in dreams. Recently she told me that while she sometimes misses being alive, she's happy she's dead because of all the trouble my sister has gone through. "I couldn't have borne it," my mother told me. "It would have made me too sad. I'd have died of sorrow."

My sister, Sarah, was the unluckiest person I ever knew, even unluckier than my father, who'd been the most unlucky until my sister started growing up. As a child Sarah had given no hint of the misfortunes she was going to experience. This only became evident after her sixteenth birthday when she went mad and had to be sent to a mental hospital. Because of her bad luck we chose a very bad hospital, where she was beaten and raped by the male nurses.

Sarah remained in that place for over six months. After she came out, she was never normal again. She got depressed or euphoric, but was so outside the boundaries of what is considered normal behaviour that she kept having to be hospitalized.

Luckily, there were better hospitals than the first one we'd sent her to, and eventually she started going on her own as a volunteer patient. When she was depressed, it affected all of us, and my mother couldn't stand it. That's why she's glad she's dead.

Sarah was unlucky because she was born at the wrong time. Nowadays if she had to go to a hospital she'd be given medication that would help lift her out of her depression. But in those days the best they could do was give electric shock.

My father had never spoken to the dead when he was alive and he made no effort to speak to the living after he died. He doesn't visit me, as my mother does, but she tells me all about him and he doesn't seem to have changed. When my mother was still alive, she explained that many people who die after the age of sixty instantly become younger at death. They return to the age they were happiest.

My father's age didn't change at death. My mother became twenty, the year she gave birth to me, which was the happiest year of her life.

Until the night before she died, at the age of sixty-four, my mother always told us that my father was a good man who became bad only when he was ill. He had been in and out of mental hospitals most of his life but his illness was different from my sister's. When she became upset, she never threatened to kill anyone, but my father became frightening, and we were in a constant state of terror as we grew up. The best thing my mother could have done was to divorce my father when my sister and I were still young. Actually, the best thing would have been not to have married him in the first place, but then Sarah and I would not have been born. This, of course, is a debatable point, whether it is better to be born with such a father. This is where luck comes in. The lucky ones find themselves with good parents; the unlucky ones with fathers like mine.

Anyway, on that evening before my mother died, she was in the hospital and I was visiting. She turned her face and said suddenly, "He isn't a good man, is he, Davie?" We stared at each other. "No, he isn't a good man," I said.

"I should have divorced him. He wasn't good for the children."

Next morning she was dead. She'd had her last heart attack and had finally been able to face the truth on her death bed. My father had not been a good man. He didn't care for people. I don't think he ever loved anything or anyone, except for one person. My mother told me that he had loved someone once long ago before he married her.

He had been married to a girl called Angel, who'd been a prostitute and who had promised him she would never go back on the street after they got married. But one of my father's brothers told him that Angel was soliciting while my father was at work, so my father divorced her.

He was ten years older than my mother, and she had fallen in love with him when she was ten. When he married Angel, my mother cried all night long. When he divorced Angel, my mother cried all night long again, this time from happiness. She was nineteen when they were married and, as I've already told you, she gave birth to me when she was twenty.

When I was fifteen she was thirty-five and very beautiful, although she had begun to put on weight. She had black, piercing eyes, jet-black hair, very long, that hung down her back, and big, friendly soft breasts. Whenever my father was in a mental hospital, she'd talk to me as if I were her husband. One night when she thought I was asleep she came into my bed and rubbed against me. I think she loved me in a way a mother is not allowed to love a son, and I think I loved her in a way a son is not allowed to love his mother. A few nights later I dreamed I was making love to her. It was a fantastic dream. I woke up terrified at what I'd done. Never in my life did I experience the ecstasy of that dream. I suspect my mother must have known about it and that this was the secret we shared. I also loved my sister, Sarah, in a way a brother is not allowed to love his sister, and my sister felt the same about me. It's easy to see we were a typical family.

My sister and I never made love, although we talked about it when we were adults and she told me she had wanted to sleep with me when she had turned sixteen. She was two years younger than I was. She wondered if that could have been the reason she had gone mad. I hope that isn't true. I denied ever wanting to sleep with her, but I was lying. I had wanted to and often I would imagine I was making love to her. But I'd been too afraid to admit it and always felt guilty.

My sister got married to a good man who loved her and they had a son, but she kept getting ill and her husband finally divorced her and was granted custody of the child. This made her even more depressed, and my mother couldn't bear it.

When my mother talked to God she was usually very angry with Him. She was convinced He hated people — why else would He make them suffer so much? I was alarmed at the disrespectful way she spoke to God and I expected Him to strike her with a shaft of lightning or a pillar of fire; but He chose to punish her by making both her husband and daughter mad.

I expressed the opinion that God was punishing her because of the way she spoke to Him, but she explained she had only started shouting and berating Him after my sister had gone crazy and after Hitler had come to power in Germany. When the H-bomb was invented, she felt she really had something to scream about. "First Hitler and then the H-bomb? And you say He doesn't hate people? Only someone who hates people would do such a thing!"

My father wasn't religious and never went to synagogue, but my mother kept a kosher house with two sets of dishes, one for milk and one for meat. She considered herself a devout Jew even though she spent so much time shouting at God. She was convinced He was responsible for everything that happened.

When my mother committed a sin, like accidentally using a milk dish for meat, or when she cursed her children or lit a fire on the Sabbath, she would pray: "Yes, oh Lord, I have sinned. I've used a milk dish for meat, and I cursed

141

my child in a fit of anger, and I lit a fire on the Sabbath. True, these are sins, but how can You compare my sins to Yours? You've killed and starved babies. You've driven people mad. What about the Nazis who killed six million Jews? It should be easy for You to forgive me, but how can I forgive you!"

Now when my mother visits me, we talk of many things, mostly of the past — how much she loved Montreal, the fun she had growing up there, her sorrows as an adult, and she still recalls the mountain in the middle of the city.

When she died she became twenty again. I think I too will become twenty when I die, so that we'll be the same age. Then she and I will finally make love, for after death everything is allowed.

About the Author

Ted Allan is the author of the award-winning screenplays, *Lies My Father Told Me* and *Love Streams*; co-author of the international bestseller, *The Scalpel, The Sword, The Story of Dr. Norman Bethune*; author of *Love Is a Long Shot*, soon to be made into a motion picture; and of the internationally published children's book, *Willie, the Squowse*, now translated into ten languages. He has earned acclaim as one of Canada's most talented and multifaceted writers.

In addition to numerous screenplays, television and radio dramas and comedies which have appeared on both the CBC and BBC during the past thirty years, seven of Allan's stage plays have been produced and acclaimed in London, Paris, Rome and other major European cities.

His short stories have appeared in *The New Yorker*, *Harper's* and other journals. He wrote his first short story, "Crazy Joe," in 1933 at the age of seventeen; and his latest, "One for the Little Boy," in 1984.

Born in Montreal, he now lives in Toronto (summers) and Los Angeles (winters) after a quarter of a century in England.